TEXAS UNIFORM COMMERCIAL CODE

Library of Congress Catalog Card Number 72-3452

ISBN 87755-173-1

Revised 1972 $2.00

Business Guide No. 12

(Revised)

TEXAS UNIFORM COMMERCIAL CODE

PRACTICAL ASPECTS ON SECURED TRANSACTIONS

GAYLORD A. JENTZ

Professor of Business Law

BUREAU OF BUSINESS RESEARCH

THE UNIVERSITY OF TEXAS AT AUSTIN

FOREWORD

The Bureau of Business Research is pleased to publish the revised edition of ***TEXAS UNIFORM COMMERCIAL CODE: PRACTICAL ASPECTS ON SECURED TRANSACTIONS*** by Gaylord A. Jentz, professor of business law, as Number 12 in its Business Guide series.

The Uniform Commercial Code became effective in the state of Texas at midnight on June 30, 1966. All secured transactions made after that date are governed by the Code. Security agreements validly entered into prior to that date will remain effective although the agreement has not been completed. These agreements are enforceable under applicable present laws, even if these laws may be modified or repealed by the Code. However, amendments required that all precode filings and security interests shall have been placed in the Code records by July 1, 1971. Dr. Jentz has prepared this guide to assist businessmen in understanding and in making effective use of secured transactions; it is not intended to be a complete statement of the law. The 60th, 61st, and 62nd legislatures made changes in the Uniform Commercial Code dealing with security interests, and these changes are reflected in this revised edition. In codification of the UCC as a part of the Business and Commerce Code, Article 9 has been changed to Chapter 9.

Bureau staff members assisting with the publication included Mrs. Linda Brenner, Robert L. Dorsett, Miss Florence Escott, Mrs. Mary Ann Gready, Robert T. Jenkins, Salvador B. Macias, Charles W. Montfort, Mrs. Margaret Robb, and Daniel P. Rosas.

Stanley A. Arbingast
Director

April 1972

CONTENTS

TEXAS UNIFORM COMMERCIAL CODE

TEXAS UNIFORM COMMERCIAL CODE: PRACTICAL ASPECTS ON SECURED TRANSACTIONS

INTRODUCTION

The purpose of Article 9, Uniform Commercial Code—Secured Transactions, is to codify and to modernize the existing law covering almost every consensual security interest in personal property, sales of accounts, contract rights, chattel paper, and the like.

Before adoption of the Uniform Commercial Code by the 59th Texas Legislature, the law was concerned primarily with who had "title" to the property and the "form" of the transaction; therefore, it was important in determining the rights of the security holder and others whether the transaction was a conditional sales contract, a chattel mortgage, a trust receipt, or some other form of security device.

The Code supersedes existing legislation dealing with these *forms* of security devices such as the Uniform Trust Receipts Act, statutes governing conditional sales and chattel mortgages (Articles 5489–99, Revised Civil Statutes of Texas, 1925, as amended), the nonnotification assignment of accounts receivable (Chapter 463, Acts of the 49th Legislature, Regular Session,

1945, as amended, compiled as Article 260–1, Vernon's Texas Civil Statutes, as amended), factor's lien statutes (Chapter 180, Acts of the 50th Legislature, Regular Session, 1947, as amended, compiled as Article 5506c, Vernon's Texas Civil Statutes, as amended), and the "goods daily exposed to sale" statute (Article 4000, Revised Civil Statutes of Texas, 1925, as amended).

The Code **does not** supersede legislation generally applicable to statutory liens and, most importantly, other legislation surrounding security transactions, such as the Interest-Consumer Credit-Consumer Protection Act (Title 79, Revised Civil Statutes of Texas, 1925, as amended, Chapter 274, Acts of the 60th Legislature, Regular Session, 1967, compiled as Article 5069, Vernon's Texas Civil Statutes).

The latter is extremely important in that any security agreement dealing with a transaction which is covered also under the Consumer Credit Code of Texas and/or the Federal Truth-In-Lending Act must comply fully with the disclosures of those acts.

Although the details of these acts are not within the purview of this monograph, a brief discussion is appropriate as compliance is essential for the secured party to avoid possible liability and to the debtor for his own protection.

The 60th Legislature of the state of Texas enacted a very comprehensive law governing permitted rates of interest and other charges encompassing all phases of the consumer-credit field. This act, in a very broad sense, places all consumer-credit transactions in some form under public regulation to be administered by a Consumer Credit Commissioner. Heretofore, only a small segment of consumer credit was regulated, principally through general interest laws and those governing small-loan licenses. The new act extends regulation to secondary mortgage loans, retail installment sales, and motor-vehicle installment sales paid on a time basis and generally permits banks and savings and loan institutions to compete on the same terms with the licensed small-loan institutions.

In addition, after many years of debate, Congress enacted and President Lyndon B. Johnson signed on May 29, 1968, what is popularly known as the Truth-In-Lending Act. The act is not intended to preempt state legislation in the credit field but to provide incentives for states to enact their own legislation and to provide a framework of credit-consumer protection in the meantime. This act does not apply to credit transactions for business or commercial purposes, and loans other than for real property of $25,000 or more are considered credit business loans and are not under the act.

The act specifically provides, "State-regulated transactions are exempt from the act if requirements are substantially the same and enforcement is provided for." There is little question that the Texas Consumer Credit Act comes closer to qualifying for the exemption from the federal regulation than most other state laws, but it does fall short in a few areas, and the Legislature has not passed legislation for full compliance. Regulation of consumer credit under the federal act is a federal-government function. Thus, in Texas, according to most observers, although consumer credit will be regulated primarily by the state, creditors must comply with both laws.

The purpose of the Truth-In-Lending law is primarily that of disclosure to those persons upon whom a finance charge is or may be imposed. The act has nothing to do with the maximum rates of interest and/or other charges which may be levied upon the borrower or buyer. These rates are provided in state statutes.

Although the Truth-In-Lending law does not apply to contracts of bailment or lease unless there is an option to buy the property and does not apply to credit for business purposes or to corporations or governments, there is no such limitation when applying the state law.

There are two terms which must be disclosed by the Truth-In-Lending law not found in the state law. They are the **finance charge** and the **annual percentage rate**.

The finance charge includes:

1. Loan fees, finder's fees, or similar charges
2. Service or carrying charges
3. Interest
4. Time price differentials
5. Investigators' fees

6. Cost of any guarantee or insurance protecting a creditor against default or credit loss

7. Any amount payable under a point, discount, or other system of additional charges

Charges or premiums for credit life, accident, or health insurance and premiums or charges for property or liability insurance where appropriate must be included in the finance charge. Other charges, such as official fees and taxes, if publicly disclosed, are not included in the finance charge.

The finance charge must be disclosed and expressed as an annual percentage rate except where (1) the finance charge is not over $5 and is applicable to an amount financed not over $75, or (2) the finance charge is not over $7.50 and is applicable to an amount financed over $75.

The annual percentage rate is the nominal annual rate determined by the actuarial method. The actuarial method is a means for computing the simple annual rate on the declining balance. The actuarial method assumes that a uniform periodic rate is applied to a schedule of installment payments such that the principal is reduced to zero upon completion of the payments. The actuarial rate is such periodic rate multiplied by the number of periods in a year. Most sellers and creditors have rate charts which they use.

The following sample chart illustrates the terminology and the requirements for disclosure. [See page 7.]

The Code is concerned principally with classifying various kinds of personal property a security interest may attach, how and where to perfect this security interest to give the best possible protection to the secured creditor as against third-party interests, and, last, to give some uniformity in remedies available upon default of the debtor. Although some may disagree, the Code has tried to take the best from the various security devices now known to businessmen and to combine them into a simplified system for the handling of secured transactions meeting the demands of modern business.

The following pages will deal with the more important aspects of Article 9 of the Uniform Commercial Code. The

PLUS	CASH PRICE	
	SALES TAX	
	(A) CASH SALE PRICE	
LESS	MERCHANDISE TRADE	
	DOWN PAYMENT	
	(B) UNPAID BALANCE OF CASH PRICE	
PLUS	TOTAL INSURANCE, OFFICIAL FEES (C) AND OTHER CHARGES AS ITEMIZED	
	(D) UNPAID BALANCE	
LESS	PREPAID FINANCE CHARGE	
	REQUIRED DEPOSIT BALANCE	
	(E) AMOUNT FINANCED	
	(F) FINANCE CHARGE	
	(G) TOTAL PAYMENTS (E) + (F) DIVIDED BY NO. OF PAYMENTS= AMOUNT OF EACH PAYMENT	
	(H) DEFERRED PAYMENT PRICE (A) + (C) + (F)	
	(I) ANNUAL PERCENTAGE RATE	

reader should be apprised that this discussion is not intended to be a complete statement of the law, but it is to be used strictly as a guideline to help the businessman understand and make effective use of secured transactions in his business. Most of the comments will refer to specific sections of the Code so that further investigation can be made as the reader deems necessary.

GENERAL COMMENTS

Article 9 of the Code does not apply to any federal statute that regulates rights of parties; landlord's liens; common law or statutory liens for services or materials; assignments of wages or compensation of employees; equipment trusts covering railroad rolling stock; sale of accounts, contracts rights, and chattel paper as part of the sale of a business or for collection only, or of contract rights to assignees who are to perform the contract; transfers of insurance claims; rights represented by judgments; rights of set-off; liens on or leases of real estate (except for fixtures); or transfers of tort claims or bank or savings accounts [§ 9.104]. The businessman will follow the same basic rules and procedures in handling these transactions as he is doing under present law.

In addition, Article 9 has limited use in remedies already provided for under other Articles of the Code. For example, under Article 2–Sales, a seller has specific remedies available to him when his buyer is in default, such as his right of resale and stoppage of goods in transit. Thus, there is no need to have a "security agreement" as defined under Article 9. Similar provisions are applied also to a security interest arising in the bank collection process. It will suffice at present simply to point out that when the seller of goods or collecting bank *rightfully obtains possession* of the goods or collection items, he automatically "perfects" his interest without the aid of Article 9 [§ 9.113, § 9.203, § 9.302(a), § 4.208].

A simple set of terminology has been created to describe the elements of the secured transactions and the parties to them. The businessman will have a standard set of terms to use regardless of the "form" of the secured transaction. These terms will appear in the security agreement, in the financing statement, and in any other relationship between the parties. The following are the most important:

1. *Secured party* relates to the former mortgagee, conditional seller, entruster, factor, assignee (of accounts) [§ 9.105 (a)(9)].

2. *Debtor* relates to the former mortgagor, conditional buyer, trustee, assignor (of accounts) [§ 9.105(a)(4)].

3. *Security interest* relates to the mortgage, "title" in conditional sales, trust receipts, factor's liens, and assignment of accounts [§ 1.201(37)].

4. *Security agreement* states the security arrangement between the parties [§ 9.105(a)(8)].

5. *Financing statement* is the instrument filed to give public notice [§ 9.402].

6. *Collateral* is the subject of the security agreement (or sale) [§ 9.105(a)(3)].

CREATION OF AN ENFORCEABLE SECURITY INTEREST

In order for the businessman to be sure that he has an enforceable security interest that attaches to the collateral, three events must occur [§ 9.203, § 9.204].

1. Unless the collateral is in the possession of the secured party, there must be a security agreement describing the collateral and signed by the debtor. (For an example of Security Agreements, see Appendix A.)

2. The secured party must give "value." In most cases, value will be any consideration to support a simple contract. It does include, also, a security for preexisting obligations and binding commitments to extend credit [§ 1.201(44)].

3. The debtor must have "rights" in the collateral. The term "rights" includes any legal interest the debtor has or will have in the collateral—except that a debtor does not have rights in crops until at least planted; young of livestock until conceived; fish until caught; oil, gas, or minerals until extracted; timber until cut; or a contract right or account until such comes into existence.

The purpose behind these three requirements is to provide an *evidentiary* basis of a legal claim by the secured party and generally to allow such security interest to flow to future, after-acquired property, or proceeds from the sale of the collateral of the debtor. Thus, the Code has validated the floating charge or lien.

PERFECTION OF THE SECURITY INTEREST

The terms of the security agreement are binding and effective as between the secured party and his debtor without perfection [§ 9.201]. The purpose of perfecting a security interest is basically to provide the secured party with a *superior* claim over the collateral as against other third parties—i.e., other secured parties of the debtor, attaching general creditors of the debtor, trustees in bankruptcy of the debtor, and purchasers of the collateral from the debtor [§ 9.301].

The secured party perfects his interest in one of three ways, depending upon the classification into which the collateral falls. In many situations, the secured party has a choice of the means of perfection, while in others there is only one method he may use. The three methods of perfection are [§ 9.302]:

1. By mere attachment at the time the security interest is created. This applies in the state of Texas to a purchase money security interest in consumer goods of any value and to a purchase money security interest in farm equipment having a purchase price not in excess of $2,500. The businessman in these situations, therefore, need not file or take possession of the collateral to get some protection. Two exceptions to the above rule apply to fixtures and motor vehicles.

2. By the transferring of possession of the collateral from the debtor to the secured party. A good example of this is a pledge.

3. By filing a financing statement. This is the most common and will be discussed later. (See Appendix B for a sample Financing Statement.)

It should be noted here that a separate document *or* a copy of the security agreement properly filed will be sufficient as a financing statement if it meets the formal requisites [§ 9.402]. These requisites are:

1. The financing statement must be signed by both debtor *and* secured party.

2. It must contain the addresses of both the debtor and the secured party.

3. It must contain a description of the type or types of collateral.

When the collateral of the security interest is crops or fixtures, additional requirements to those above must be met [§ 9.402(a)]. (See page 13.)

TYPES OF COLLATERAL AND SPECIFIC MEANS OF PERFECTING A SECURITY INTEREST

The Code is *not* concerned with the "form" of the transaction as to the means of perfection. Perfection under the Code is dependent upon the types of collateral which are the basis of the security agreement.

The two general categories or types of personal property governed by Article 9 are (1) tangible property or "goods" and (2) intangible property. To afford a better understanding of intangible property, in this discussion this category is broken down even further to include a classification called "indispensable paper." The reasons for this will be demonstrated in a chart which will follow.

Familiarity with the definitions of types of collateral within each of the general classifications above is essential to the understanding of the Code. If filing is to be the means of perfection, the businessman will soon see that *where* to file will depend upon the classification and that, should he file elsewhere, he may lose his security interest in the collateral. In Texas, filing will be either centrally with the Secretary of State or locally with the County Clerk [§ 9.401]. Although this is an oversimplification, a general rule of thumb is that all filing should be centrally with the Secretary of State, except those security transactions which deal with consumer goods or pertain to the business of the farmer. The latter should filed locally.

Determining that the borrower is a farmer, merchant, or consumer is *not* enough to classify the collateral. The determination is dependent on the *use* being made or to be made of the collateral. The use concept is new and places an additional burden on the businessman, banks, and lending institutions that they did not have under the former law. For example, a refrigerator would be a consumer good if sold to a householder; inventory in the hands of a merchant selling appliances; equipment if used by a restaurant; and farm equipment if used to store eggs, etc., for resale. In each of the above, the key to the classification was the use being made of this same refrigerator.

Occasionally, a "good" may be used for more than one purpose. For example, a bulldozer could be used by the owner in a farming operation and in the road-building business. Under these circumstances, it becomes a question of the *primary use* being made of the property as to its classification and, thus, its filing. Once properly filed, a change in the use of the collateral does not impair the security interest of the secured party [§ 9.401(c)].

Tangible Goods

There are certain secured transactions wherein the collateral consists of *tangible goods* that involve considerations in perfecting a security interest other than the use concept.

1. *Crops.* If the collateral is crops grown by a resident debtor, the financing statement must be filed with the County Clerk in the county of the debtor's residence *and* in the county where the land on which the crops are growing or are to be grown is located. Frequently, this will require only one filing where the debtor's residence and land on which crops are growing are one and the same [§ 9.401(a)(1)]. To have a proper filing, the financing statement relating to crops must contain *both* a general description of the real estate on which the crops are growing or are to be grown *and* the name of the record owner of the realty. The purpose of this latter requirement is to provide a party searching the Code records with additional identification of the real estate upon which the crops are or will be grown [§ 9.402(a),(c)].

2. *Fixtures.* If the collateral is or is to become a fixture, the financing statement must be filed in the office of the County Clerk in the county where the real estate concerned is located [§ 9.401(a)(2)]. After June 18, 1967, to perfect properly a security interest in fixtures, the financing statement must

include (1) a description of the real estate concerned *and* the name of the record owner thereof and (2) the statement "Collateral is or includes fixtures," or its substantial equivalent [§ 9.402(a),(c)]. Should either of these requirements not be met, a secured party obtains only a perfected security interest in chattels other than the fixtures covered in the financing statement. The Code affords some relief in applying these requirements where the fixture financing statement incorrectly identifies the name of the record owner [§ 9.402(a)].

> Where the financing statement relates to a purchase money security interest in fixtures having a purchase price not in excess of $1,500, the requirement that the financing statement contain the name of the record owner is satisfied by using the name supplied by the debtor, unless the secured party knows that this name is not that of the record owner. The party attacking the effectiveness of a filing has the burden of establishing that the secured party knew at the time he filed the financing statement that the name entered on the financing statement was not that of the record owner.

A financing statement meeting the above requirements perfects *only* a security interest in fixtures. Should the collateral consist partly of fixtures and partly of goods other than fixtures, *two* separate financing statements have to be properly filed [§ 9.403(d)].

Each County Clerk is required to create and maintain a separate index book for fixture financing statements endorsed "Security Interests in Fixtures." This means that in searching the Code records in the office of the County Clerk, financing statements covering fixtures will not be indexed with financing statements covering other forms of collateral. Each financing statement shall be indexed by the Clerk under the name of the debtor [§ 9.403(d)]. It has been recommended by the Secretary of State, in the case of fixtures, that the financing statement also be indexed under the name of the record owner when it differs from that of the debtor and that the parties be so identified as "nonowner" and "record owner," respectively.

3. *Nonresident debtors*. Where the collateral is equipment used in farming operations, farm products, or consumer goods

and where the debtor is a nonresident, the financing statement is filed where the goods are kept [§ 9.401(a)(1)].

4. *Equipment used in more than one state or jurisdiction.* If the collateral consists of types of goods which normally are used in more than one jurisdiction (such as automotive equipment, rolling stock, airplanes, road-building equipment, commercial harvesting equipment, construction machinery, and the like) and if these goods are classified as equipment or as inventory by reason of their being leased by the debtor to others, then if the debtor's chief place of business is *not* in the state of Texas, the law of Texas will *not* apply to the transaction *unless* his chief place of business is located in a jurisdiction which does not provide for the perfection of a security interest by filing or recording [§ 9.103(b)]. Since all states, except Louisiana, have adopted the Uniform Commercial Code, it will be hard to find any state that does not provide for filing or recording. Also, for the purpose of determining the validity and perfection of a security interest in an airplane, the chief place of business of a debtor who is a foreign air carrier under the Federal Aviation Act of 1958, as amended, is the designated office of the agent upon whom service of process may be made on behalf of the debtor.

5. *Collateral brought into the state of Texas.* The validity of a security interest on all collateral *not* covered in paragraph (4) above, which is brought into this state already subject to a security interest, is determined by the law of the jurisdiction where the property was when the security interest attached. There is an exception to this rule. Where it is understood by the parties to the transaction *at the time the security interest attached* that the collateral would be kept in the state of Texas *and* the collateral is actually brought into this state within thirty (30) days thereafter for purposes other than transportation through the state, the law of the state of Texas is applicable.

A security interest perfected in another jurisdiction remains perfected in the state of Texas for a period of four (4) months and continues thereafter only if filed in the state of Texas during the four-month period. If filed after the four-month period, the perfection takes effect only from the date of such filing [§ 9.103(c)].

6. *Change of residence or location of collateral within the state of Texas as to local filing.* A filing which is made in the proper county continues effective for four (4) months after a change to another county of the debtor's residence or location of the collateral, whichever controlled the original filing after this period. The perfection becomes ineffective after this period unless a copy of the financing statement *signed* by the secured party is filed in the new county within this period. The security interest can be perfected after the four-month period by filing, but the perfection dates only from the time of this filing [§ 9.401(3)]. Thus, a security interest filed in Travis County on farm products located in that county would remain perfected without filing when moved to Harris County for a period of four (4) months.

7. *Certificate of title laws.* In the state of Texas, to perfect a security interest on a motor vehicle (unless such is held as inventory) which is the subject of a "*first sale*" (or subsequent sale) is by *notation* on the certificate of title [§ 9.103(d), § 9.302(c)(2); Vernon's Texas Penal Code, Article 1436–1, § 41–§ 47a]. Where the collateral is a motor vehicle held as inventory, the security interest must be perfected by filing centrally with the Secretary of State [§ 9.302(a),(c),(d)]. It should be noted that the Code defines inventory to include a motor vehicle for lease as well as for sale [§ 9.109(4)]. The security interest, once properly perfected, however, will not affect the ordinary purchaser who buys a motor vehicle in good faith from an auto dealer [§ 9.307(a)]. (See page 25 for details.)

Intangibles

As a general rule, where the collateral consists of intangibles, all filing is required to be *centrally* with the Secretary of State, with the following exceptions:

1. *Instruments.* A security interest in instruments, other than instruments which constitute part of a chattel paper such as a chattel mortgage, can be perfected *only* by the secured party taking possession. There is an exception in which a secured party has protection without possession for 21 days, under limited circumstances. This latter exception also applies to documents of title [§ 9.304(a),(d),(e)].

2. *Farmers.* Accounts, contract rights, and general intangibles arising from or relating to the sale of farm products by a farmer are filed in the county of the residence of the debtor if he is a resident of the state of Texas and, if a nonresident, in the county where the farm products are kept [§ 9.401(a)(1)].

3. *Location of records of accounts or contract rights.* If the assignor of accounts or contract rights keeps his records concerning them outside the state of Texas, the law of that state applies where such office is located [§ 9.103(a)].

4. *Debtor's chief place of business concerning general intangibles.* If the chief place of business of a debtor is outside the state of Texas, the validity and perfection of a security interest in intangibles is governed by the law of that jurisdiction unless that jurisdiction does not provide for perfection by filing or recording, and then the law of Texas will apply [§ 9.103(b)].

5. *Intangible collateral brought into the state of Texas.* Chattel paper and documents which are subject to a security interest when brought into this state other than for transportation through the state are governed by the law of the state where they were located when the security interest attached, unless at the time the security interest attached the parties understood that they were to be kept in the state of Texas and they are brought into this state within thirty (30) days thereafter. A security interest perfected in another jurisdiction will remain effective for a period of four (4) months in the state of Texas and will continue, if filed in this state, during that period of time. After the four-month period is up, the security interest may be filed, but perfection will take effect only from the date of such filing [§ 9.103(c)].

6. *Change of residence or location within the state of Texas.* A filing of accounts, contract rights, or other general

intangibles arising from the sale of farm products by a resident farmer continues in effect for four (4) months after a change of the debtor's residence to another county. If the secured party files a copy of the financing statement *signed* by the secured party in the new county during the four-month period, the security interest, as perfected, continues. If the four-month period expires, the secured party loses his perfected interest in the new county unless he files again, and then his perfection takes effect at the time of the later filing [§ 9.401(c)].

The following pages will define the various classifications of the collateral, will discuss how to perfect such security interest, and will give some brief comments concerning each. The chart is not intended as a substitute for the Code or the advice of counsel but rather as a general reference to the filing and other provisions applicable to the ordinary secured transaction.

EFFECT OF THE UNPERFECTED SECURITY INTEREST

The general purpose of perfecting a security interest is to gain protection so that the secured party's security interest is enforceable as against third-party interests in the same collateral. It should be obvious to the businessman that the unperfected interest is of very low quality in disputes with third parties [§ 9.301].

For example, a secured party who perfected properly his security interest would prevail over a secured party who failed to perfect his interest, assuming both are nonpurchase money advances. Suppose A lends B $500 and takes a chattel mortgage on a prize bull belonging to B. A does not perfect his interest. X Bank later lends B $500 with B signing a chattel mortgage on

FILING CHART FOR SECURED TRANSACTIONS IN TEXAS

Classification of collateral	Central filing—Secretary of State	Local filing—county of debtor's residence or, if nonresident, where goods are kept	Definitions and comments
I. Tangible goods 1. Equipment	X [§9.401(a)(3)]		(a) Goods are "equipment" if they are used or bought for use primarily in business (exclude farming for filing purposes only here) or by a debtor who is a nonprofit organization or a governmental subdivision or agency or if the goods are not included in definitions of inventory, farm products, or consumer goods [§9.109(2)]. (b) Note previous discussion on business equipment used in more than one jurisdiction *and* that this Section does not apply to motor vehicles.
2. Farm equipment	(By attachment without filing or taking of possession on purchase money security interest with purchase price not in excess of $2,500) [§9.302(a)(3)]	All others X [§9.401(a)(1)]	(a) Goods are "farm equipment" when used or bought for use primarily in the farming business or farming operation. Farming operation or business is not defined, but some help can be had from the definition of farm products which follows [§9.109(2)(3)]. (b) Note particularly previous discussion on changing location of collateral or debtor's residence to a different county.

Classification of collateral	Central filing—Secretary of State	Local filing—county of debtor's residence or, if nonresident, where goods are kept	Definitions and comments
3. Farm products		X [§9.401(a)(1)] (also: if the collateral is crops, then with the County Clerk in the county where the land on which such crops are growing or are to be grown is located)	(a) Goods are "farm products" if they are crops or livestock or supplies used or produced in farming operations or if they are products of crops or livestock in their unmanufactured state (such as ginned cotton, maple syrup, milk, and eggs) and if they are in the possession of a debtor engaged in raising, fattening, grazing, or other farm operations. If goods are farm products, they are neither equipment nor inventory [§9.109(3)]. (b) Note later discussion governing the time when the security interest attaches to crops and the priorities in regard to such.
4. Consumer goods	(By attachment without filing or taking of possession on a purchase money security interest) [§9.302(a)(4)]	All others X [§9.401(a)(1)]	(a) Goods are "consumer goods" if they are used or bought for use primarily for personal, family, or household purposes [§9.109(1)]. (b) Note particularly previous discussion on changing location of collateral or debtor's residence to a different county; also, that this does not apply to motor vehicles.
5. Inventory	X [§9.401(a)(3)]		(a) Goods are "inventory" if they are held by a person who holds them for sale or lease or to be furnished under contracts of service, or if he has so furnished

Classification of collateral	Central filing–Secretary of State	Local filing–county of debtor's residence or, if nonresident, where goods are kept	Definitions and comments
			them, or if they are raw materials, work in process or materials used or consumed in a business. Inventory of a person is not to be classified as his equipment [§9.109(4)]. (b) In Texas, a security interest in a motor vehicle in a dealer's inventory is perfected by filing centrally, as notation on the certificate of title applies only to "first sale" or a subsequent sale.
6. Fixtures (goods affixed to real estate)		(Office of the County Clerk in the county where the real estate concerned is located. See page 13 for important details in filing requirements.) [§9.401(a)(2)]	(a) The term "fixtures" is not defined by the Code but consists generally of personal property which is attached to real estate in some permanent fashion and intended to be a part of the realty. No security interest exists in goods incorporated into a structure in the manner of lumber, bricks, tile, cement, glass, metal, and the like unless the structure remains personal property [§9.313(a)]. (b) Because of the difficulty of determining whether some articles of personal property are to become fixtures, the maximum protection may be secured by filing in the office of the County Clerk in the county where the real estate concerned is located [§9.401(a)(2)] *and* also according to their other possible classification such as consumer goods, business equipment, farm equipment, and the like. (See page 14 for details.)

Classification of collateral	Central filing—Secretary of State	Local filing—county of debtor's residence or, if nonresident, where goods are kept	Definitions and comments
7. Accessions	(Filing is determined by the classification of the goods to which these goods are attached)		(a) Goods are "accessions" if they are to be installed in or affixed to other goods [§9.314(a)]. (b) An example would be installing a new engine in a tractor used on a farm. Since accessories are to be installed in or affixed to other goods and will partake of the nature of said goods, the place of filing depends on the classification of the goods in which they are installed or to which they are affixed. They may be farm equipment, consumer goods, inventory, etc., and the place of filing is determined accordingly.
II. Intangibles 1. Indispensable paper A. Chattel paper	X [§9.401(a)(3)] (Can also perfect by taking possession)		(a) "Chattel paper" is defined as a writing or writings which evidence both a monetary obligation and a security interest in or a lease of specific goods; a charter or other contract involving the use or hire of a vessel is not chattel paper. When a transaction is evidenced both by such a security agreement or a lease *and* by an instrument or series of instruments, the group of writings taken together constitutes chattel paper [§9.105(a)(2)]. This includes dealer paper, such as notes, chattel mortgages, and conditional sales contracts.

Classification of collateral	Central filing—Secretary of State	Local filing—county of debtor's residence or, if nonresident, where goods are kept	Definitions and comments
			(b) Where chattel paper is left in the hands of the assignor, a purchaser for value in the ordinary course of business takes good title free of the security interest under certain cirsumstances [§9.308]. It is for this reason that maximum security is perfected by the assignee taking possession of the chattel paper [§9.305].
B. Instruments	(Possession only perfects—*no* filing)		(a) "Instrument" means a negotiable instrument (defined in another Section of the Code [§3.104]) or an investment "security" [§8.102] or any other writing which evidences a right to the payment of money and is not itself a security agreement or lease and is of a type which is in the ordinary course of business transferred by delivery with any necessary indorsement or assignment [§9.105(a)(7)]. (b) A security interest in instruments (other than instruments which constitute a part of chattel paper) can be perfected only by the secured party's taking possession, and filing provisions do not apply [§9.304(a)]. However, under certain cirsumstances, the secured party has limited protection for twenty-one (21) days without possession [§9.304(d)(e)].

Classification of collateral	Central filing—Secretary of State	Local filing—county of debtor's residence or, if nonresident, where goods are kept	Definitions and comments
C. Documents	X [§9.401(a)(3)] (Can also perfect by taking possession)		(a) "Document of title" includes bills of lading, dock warrants, dock receipts, warehouse receipts or order for delivery of goods, and also any other document which in the regular course of business or financing is treated as adequately evidencing that the person in possession of it is entitled to receive, hold, and dispose of the document and the goods it covers. To be a document of title, a document must purport to be issued by or addressed to a bailee and purport to cover goods in the bailee's possession which either are identified or are fungible portions of an identified mass [§1.201(15)]. (b) Documents may be *negotiable*, and, if so, the maximum perfection afforded to the secured party would be *only* by possession and *not* by filing [§9.309].
2. Accounts receivable (a) Nonfarm: accounts other than those arising from or relating	X [§9.401(a)(3)]		(a) "Account" means any right to payment for goods sold or leased for services rendered which is *not* evidenced by an instrument or chattel paper [§9.106]. (b) The account must be due and owing to distinguish it from the rights under a contract which has not been performed.

Classification of collateral	Central filing—Secretary of State	Local filing—county of debtor's residence or, if nonresident, where goods are kept	Definitions and comments
to the sale of farm products by a farmer. (b) Farm: accounts arising from or relating to the sale of farm products by a farmer.	X [§9.401(a)(3)]	X [§9.401(a)(1)]	(c) Filing is not required where the assignment is of accounts which do not alone or in conjunction with other assignments to the *same* assignee transfer a significant part of the outstanding accounts of the assignor [§9.302(a)(5)]. Isolated or casual assignments of accounts do *not* have to be filed, but any person who *regularly* takes assignments of any debtor's accounts should file. (d) Note previous discussion on application of Texas law as to place where records of debtor's accounts are kept and change of address of farmer debtor. (e) Does not apply to all rights earned or unearned under or incidental to a charter or other contract involving the use or hire of a vessel.
3. Contract rights (a) Nonfarm: contract rights other than those arising from or			(a) "Contract right" means any right to payment under a contract not yet earned by peformance and not evidenced by an instrument or chattel paper [§9.106]. For example, a construction contract, where the contractor's right to payment is made periodically at various stages of construction, is a "contract right." (b) *Contract rights* become *accounts* as performance takes place and as the right to payment is earned. Note the similarity of filing for perfection.

Classification of collateral	Central filing—Secretary of State	Local filing—county of debtor's residence or, if nonresident, where goods are kept	Definitions and comments
relating to the sale of farm products by a farmer (b) Farm: contract rights arising from or relating to the sale of farm products by a farmer.	X [§9.401(a)(3)]	X [§9.401(a)(1)]	(c) Filing is not required where the assignment is of contract rights which do not alone or in conjunction with other assignments to the same assignee transfer a significant part of the outstanding contract rights of the assignor [§9.302(a)(5)]. See prior discussion as applicable to accounts. (d) Note previous discussion on application of Texas law as to place where records of debtor's contracts are kept and change of address of farmer debtor. (e) Applies to all rights earned or unearned under or incidental to a charter or other contract involving the use or hire of a vessel.
4. General intangibles (a) Nonfarm: general intangibles other than			(a) "General intangibles" means any personal property (including things in action) other than goods, accounts, contract rights, chattel paper, documents, and instruments [§9.106]. Examples are goodwill, literary rights, trademarks, patents, copyrights, and the

Classification of collateral	Central filing—Secretary of State	Local filing—county of debtor's residence or, if nonresident, where goods are kept	Definitions and comments
those arising from or relating to the sale of farm products by a farmer.	X [§9.401(a)(3)]		like. Thus, the Code brings under this Section miscellaneous types of contractual rights and other personal property which are used as commercial security.
			(b) Note previous discussion concerning applicability of Texas laws to a security interest perfected where the chief place of debtor's business is located.
(b) Farm: general intangibles arising from or relating to the sale of farm products by a farmer.		X [§9.401(a)(1)]	(c) Does not apply to all rights earned or unearned under or incidental to a charter or other contract involving the use or hire of a vessel.

this same bull. Should X Bank file or take possession of the bull first, the bank takes priority, even though A's contract was first in time, and it makes no difference whether or not the X Bank knows of the other interest at the time it perfects its own interest [§ 9.312(e)].

Another example is a "lien creditor" who, *without knowledge* of the unperfected interest, prevails over such an interest [§ 9.301(a)(2)]. A "lien creditor" is broadly defined in the Code to include not only creditors who have acquired a lien on the property involved by attachment, levy, or the like but assignees for benefit of creditors, trustees in bankruptcy, and receivers in equity [§ 9.301(c)].

Similarly, buyers (other than secured parties) of goods, instruments, documents, and chattel paper prevail over an unperfected security interest *if they give value and take delivery without knowledge* before the interest is perfected [§ 9.301 (a)(3) and § 9.307(b)]. This same rule applies to accounts, contract rights, and general intangibles as previously defined, with the obvious exception of no need for the buyer to take delivery.

The importance of perfecting a security interest cannot be overstressed. Too often the secured party is content to rely solely upon the terms and conditions of the security agreement which he has made with his debtor. Although such a security agreement is legally binding between the secured party and the debtor, it is the unknown third party interest that may siphon away the secured party's interest upon the debtor's default. Often the difference between recovery and loss may lie in a secured party properly perfecting his security interest.

PROTECTION GIVEN TO BUYERS OF GOODS, PURCHASERS OF CHATTEL PAPER, AND HOLDERS OF NEGOTIABLE AND NONNEGOTIABLE INSTRUMENTS AND DOCUMENTS

Occasionally, perfecting a security interest will not protect a secured party as against *certain third parties*. The Code deems it more important to protect these third parties than the secured party. The following paragraphs will discuss these groups and illustrate situations in which the third-party interest prevails over the perfected security interest.

One such class that the Code protects is the buyers of goods. A buyer in the *ordinary course of business*, other than a person buying farm products from a person engaged in farming operations, takes free of a security interest created by his seller even though the security interest is *perfected* and even though the buyer *knows* of its existence [§ 9.307(a)].

The key to the above is the definition of a "buyer in the ordinary course of business." The Code defines such a person as one who, in good faith and without knowledge that the sale to him is in violation of the ownership rights or security interest of a third party in the goods, buys in the ordinary course from a person in the business of selling goods of that kind [§ 1.201(9)]. This does not include a pawnbroker.

The average consumer who buys goods from a merchant should not be subject to nor required to find out if there is an outstanding security interest on the *inventory* of the merchant. The Code even goes further and provides that the consumer will prevail over this perfected security interest even if the consumer knows of the existence of this interest at the time of sale. The consumer will not prevail, however, if he knows the sale is in violation of some term in the security agreement which is not waived by the words or conduct of the secured party. One word of caution here is that, in other states, decisions under the Code have held that cattle in possession of a farmer are considered farm products and *not inventory*. In this instance, a buyer in the ordinary course of business would *not* prevail over a secured party who had perfected his security interest.

To illustrate the above, assume that M (merchant in the appliance business) seeks a loan from B (bank), putting up his inventory of refrigerators, stoves, freezers, and other appliances as security for the loan. The bank, B, perfects its security interest by filing a financing statement centrally with the Secretary of State of Texas. A week after all this is done, C (consumer) visits M's store, wishing to purchase a new freezer. If C purchases this freezer, in which B already has a security interest, B will lose his security interest in this freezer even though C knew that the bank had filed. The only way that B could prevail over C would be to prove that C knew he bought in violation of some term in the security agreement between B and M and that B has not authorized the sale by M.

Another class of buyer, which has been referred to as "the next-door-neighbor buyer," as he does not buy in the ordinary course of business as defined above, receives some protection as against the secured party who has the automatic perfected purchase money security interest by attachment in consumer goods and farm equipment having an original purchase price not in excess of $2,500.

When dealing with a purchase money security interest in consumer goods or farm equipment having a purchase price not in excess of $2,500, an automatic perfected interest becomes effective without filing or taking possession of the collateral [§ 9.302(a)(3)(4)]. This perfection is good against all third parties *except* the buyer from the debtor *if* the following conditions have been met [§ 9.307(b)]:

1. The buyer must buy without knowledge of the security interest.
2. He must give value (as previously defined).
3. The purchase must be either for the buyer's own personal, family, or household purposes *or* for equipment to be used for his own farming operations.

4. The purchase must take place *before* the secured party files a financing statement.

Assume M (merchant in the appliance business) sells a freezer out of his inventory to C (consumer) either on a conditional sales contract or chattel mortgage as C cannot pay the full purchase price. Since this is a purchase money security interest in consumer goods, filing is not necessary for the secured party, M, to perfect his interest, and M does not do so. C takes the freezer home but does not like the style as well as does his friend, N, who purchases the freezer without knowledge of M's security interest. If C defaults, M has lost his security interest in the freezer and becomes a general creditor of C, since N has met the above requirements and would prevail.

How could the secured party, M, have prevailed over N? Of course, M would prevail if N had knowledge of M's interest, or N had not given value, or N had purchased the freezer other than for his own use—such as for resale. These events are unlikely in the average transaction. Thus, the primary method by which M would prevail is by filing his security interest before C sold the freezer to N [§ 9.307(b)].

Another class of buyers which receives some protection as against a secured party who has perfected his security interest are the purchasers of chattel paper and nonnegotiable instruments. To simplify the explanation of the extent of this protection, it is desirable to discuss each class of collateral separately.

Arrangements where the chattel paper is delivered to the assignee of the secured party, who then makes collections, as well as arrangements where the secured party, whether or not he is left in possession of the paper, makes the collections are both widely used and are known, respectively, as notification (or "direct collection") and nonnotification (or "indirect collection") arrangements. In the automobile field, for example, when a car is sold to a consumer-buyer under an installment purchase agreement and the resulting chattel paper is assigned, the assignee usually takes possession, and the obligor is notified of the assignment and is directed to make payments to the assignee. In the furniture field, on the other hand, the chattel paper may be left in the dealer's hands or delivered to the assignee; in either case, the obligor usually is not notified, and payments are made to the dealer-assignor who receives them under a duty to remit to his assignee. The widespread use of both methods of dealing with chattel paper is recognized by the provisions of Article 9 which permit perfection of a chattel paper security interest either by filing or by taking possession.

Where perfection is made by filing, a purchaser who gives *new value* and takes *possession* of it in the *ordinary course* of his business without knowledge that the chattel paper is subject to a security interest has priority. It is obvious that the keys to this protection are primarily that the purchaser take possession in the ordinary course of his business and that he is without knowledge. The secured party will prevail if he keeps possession or, because of the knowledge requirement, if he wishes to leave the paper in the debtor's possession and protect himself by stamping or noting on the paper the fact that it has been assigned to him [§ 9.308].

In addition, a purchaser of chattel paper who gives new value and takes possession of the paper in the ordinary course of his business has priority over a perfected security interest in chattel paper which is claimed merely as "proceeds" of *inventory* subject to this security interest, *even though* the purchaser has *knowledge* of this outstanding interest. More will be said on proceeds later.

A security interest in an instrument, whether negotiable or nonnegotiable, cannot be perfected by filing. (See filing chart.) The only type of perfected nonpossessory security interest that can arise in an instrument is a temporary twenty-one (21) day perfection allowed under limited circumstances—such as delivery to the debtor for purpose of collection [§ 9.304(d),(e),(f)]. The same rules apply here as to chattel paper *except* as to the rule on "proceeds" which is only applicable to chattel paper [§ 9.308].

The last class of purchasers afforded protection as against a security interest are the purchasers of *negotiable* instruments and documents referred to as holders in due course or bona fide purchasers for value. The existing law in Texas concerning these parties is relatively unchanged, and it will suffice here simply to say that they will have priority over an earlier security interest even though perfected [§ 9.309].

PRIORITIES AMONG SECURED PARTIES WITH PERFECTED INTERESTS IN THE SAME COLLATERAL

In a variety of situations, two or more persons may claim an interest in the same property. When this happens, there is obviously a conflict when the debtor is in default, and the businessman should consult his attorney immediately. To assist the businessman in determining priorities, some general rules should be discussed.

Generally, unless the collateral is under a purchase money security interest or deals with a perfected security interest in crops, the first secured party to perfect prevails over a later perfection by another secured party on the same collateral, and, once perfected, the priority applies to later subsequent advances. If neither security interest is perfected, then the first security interest to attach prevails [§ 9.312].

Although somewhat of an oversimplification, perhaps an illustration would help. A, a secured party, has a security agreement with X, debtor, on his inventory, and A files a financing statement on March 1. On April 1, B extends credit to X, signing a nonpurchase security agreement covering the same collateral as A's security interest. B files a financing statement that same day. On May 1, B advances X additional credit covering the same collateral, and, on May 20, A advances additional credit. X now defaults, and the question is which security interest, A or B, will prevail and to what extent? The answer under the Code is that A will prevail to the extent of not only his original security interest but to the subsequent advance made on May 20. This would apply even though B's subsequent advance was first in time and even though A might know of B's security interest at the time he made the May 20 advance.

Since the *time* of perfection is so important in dealing with priority of claims, a brief outline of the moment perfection takes place is appropriate. As explained previously, there are three means of perfection: attachment, possession, and filing. Where perfection is by attachment, it is perfected as soon as the secured party makes a security agreement and gives value and the debtor acquires an interest in the collateral. Where perfection is by possession, the perfection dates from the time possession is taken and continues as long as possession is retained. Where perfection is by filing, the perfection dates from the time of filing. The Code allows a secured party to file before the security interest attaches, and in such a case the security interest is perfected at the time of attachment rather than at the time of filing [§ 9.303].

The purchase money security interest does gain some priority when dealing with conflicting claims. A purchase money security interest is defined in the Code as either an interest taken or retained by the seller of the collateral to serve all or part of the purchase price *or* taken by a person who, by making advances or incurring an obligation, gives value to *enable* the debtor to acquire rights in or the use of collateral *if* such value is in fact so used [§ 9.107]. An example would be B, who wants to purchase a washer from A but does not have sufficient cash to pay all of the purchase price. A transfers the washer to B, by B making a down payment and giving A a security interest in the washer for the balance. This would be a purchase money security interest. Also, for example, if X Bank lent B the money to purchase the washer, taking a chattel mortgage on the washer, and B so applied the funds to the purchase, the X Bank would have a purchase money security interest.

The Code gives priority to a purchase money security interest *in inventory* over a nonpurchase money security under limited conditions, designed primarily to be asserted as against after-acquired property clauses [§ 9.312(c)]. As to purchase money security interests in other forms of collateral outside of inventory, the purchase money security interest takes priority provided that this interest is perfected when the debtor receives possession of the collateral or within ten (10) days thereafter [§ 9.312(d)]. If the secured party *files* within this ten-day period or before, he takes priority over the rights of a transferee in bulk or a lien creditor's interest which arose between the time the security interest attached and the time of filing [§ 9.301(b)].

THE PERFECTED INTEREST AS IT APPLIES TO AFTER-ACQUIRED PROPERTY, FUTURE ADVANCES, "PROCEEDS," AND COMMINGLED GOODS

Except in two specific instances, the Code accepts and perpetuates the concept of the "floating lien." It is for this reason that a security agreement may provide that collateral, *whenever acquired*, shall secure all obligations covered by the security agreement [§ 9.204(c)]. In addition, *providing* the security agreement so states, the collateral may secure *future* as well as present advances [§ 9.204(e)]. The interest in after-acquired property and future advances dates from the time of original perfection [§ 9.312(e),(f)]. These provisions will be standard equipment in the security agreement forms used by the businessman and will appear in the financing statement filed.

The following illustration combines the above and previous sections. Assume that A (secured party) extends credit to X (debtor) under a security agreement which covers "all the equipment in X's plant" and contains an after-acquired property clause. The agreement is made on June 1 and filed centrally with the Secretary of State of Texas that same date. On June 15, X acquires a new piece of equipment, and B (another secured party) makes an advance on this particular piece of equipment, signing a security agreement, and properly files his interest that same date. On June 30, A, under the original security agreement of June 1, makes an advance against this same particular piece of equipment acquired June 15. Should X be in default, which of the secured parties, A or B, has priority as to the piece of equipment acquired on June 15?

The answer would depend upon whether B's advance created a purchase money security interest. In the previous section, a purchase money security interest in collateral other than inventory gave the secured party priority over A's nonpurchase money interest providing B's interest attached before X received possession or within ten days thereafter. B's filing on June 15 would give him priority. If, however, B's advance is not a purchase money security interest, A's interest in the June 15 advancement will prevail. The original security interest provided for after-acquired and future advances, and, thus, the time of priority for such dates back to the original time of perfection, which in our illustration is June 1.

There are two exceptions applied to the after-acquired property clause. The first deals with crops which are to be grown *more* than three (3) years from the time the security agreement is executed. This follows the standard concept of prohibiting long-term security agreements to cover future crops, although the period is longer in Texas than in most states. There is an exception even to this rule to allow a longer time sequence where such security interest is in conjunction with a lease, land purchase, or land improvement contractual obligation [§ 9.204(d)(1)]. The second exception states that after-acquired property clauses are not effective as to consumer goods (except accessions) *unless* the debtor acquired rights in them within ten

(10) days after the secured party gave value. After the ten-day period, the after-acquired property clause is completely ineffective [§ 9.204(d)(2)].

A security interest which also applies to "proceeds" includes whatever is received when collateral or proceeds are sold, exchanged, collected, or otherwise disposed of. "Cash proceeds" includes checks, money, and the like. All other proceeds are "noncash proceeds" [§ 9.306(a)]. The purpose of including such a right to proceeds in both the security agreement and the financing statement is to allow the secured party to reclaim the proceeds, upon the sale of the collateral subject to his security interest, in the hands of the debtor or the debtor's trustee in bankruptcy.

The security interest of the secured party continues in the original collateral, even in the hands of third parties if the sale to them is *unauthorized* either by law or by agreement [§ 9.306(b)]. This means that the transferee takes subject to the security interest, and the secured party may repossess the collateral from him or in an appropriate case maintain an action for conversion.

In many cases, a purchaser or other transferree of the collateral takes free of the security interest of the secured party, and in these cases the secured party's only right will be to the proceeds. It is important to the businessman to provide for his security interest to cover proceeds, and, in describing the collateral, the word "proceeds" is sufficient to be included without further description [§ 9.203(a)(2)].

The security interest in proceeds is a *continuously* perfected interest. If, however, the *original financing* statement does not claim proceeds, a second financing statement must be filed within ten (10) days after the receipt of the proceeds by the debtor, or the secured party loses his interest in those proceeds [§ 9.306(c)]. For this reason, when filing the form used in perfecting the original security interest, the form should include in the description the word "proceeds."

Should insolvency proceedings be instituted either by or against the debtor, the general rule is that the secured party has a right to the *undeposited* cash proceeds or noncash proceeds as long as such are identifiable to the secured party's interest [§ 9.306(d)]. If the cash proceeds have been deposited in a bank account or commingled, the secured party's right is limited to the amounts received by the debtor within ten (10) days prior to such insolvency proceedings, without the requirement of identification *but* reduced by the amount received by the debtor *and* paid to the secured party during this ten-day period. This is subject to any right of set-off [§ 9.306(d)].

In certain business operations, goods, on which there has already been filed a perfected security interest, are commingled with other goods and become a part of the product or mass. The question frequently asked is what happens to this security interest upon such commingling. The Code provides that the security interest continues in the product or mass *if* the goods lose their identity in processing or manufacturing or the financing statement covering the original goods also covers the product into which the goods have been manufactured or processed [§ 9.315(a)]. If this happens and *more than one* security interest attaches to the product or mass, they rank equally according to the cost ratio of their contribution to the total mass [§ 9.315(b)].

It is obvious from the previous discussion that the rules relating to after-acquired property, future advances, commingled or processed goods, and proceeds make possible for a lien on a shifting stock of goods called the "floating lien." It is, therefore, possible for a lien to begin with raw materials, pass to work in process, to finished inventory, to accounts receivable or chattel paper, and to any cash proceeds under one perfected security interest [§ 9.205].

FILING INFORMATION AND FEES

As pointed out earlier, a financing statement is sufficient if it is signed by both the debtor and creditor, gives the address of the secured party from whom information concerning the security interest may be obtained, gives the mailing address of the debtor, and contains a statement indicating the types, or describing the items, of collateral. Also, if the collateral is crops or fixtures, the financing statement must contain a description of the real property concerned and the name of the record owner of the realty [§ 9.402]. Minor errors, which are *not* misleading, do *not* affect the validity or effect of the filing [§ 9.402(e)]. Care should always be taken to obtain the necessary information accurately, and the businessman should not rely upon the Code to save the validity of his filing.

The security interest is perfected by filing when the financing statement is presented to the filing officer *and* when the filing fee is tendered *or* the financing statement is accepted by the filing officer [§ 9.403(a)]. The fee is $3.00 [§ 9.403(e)] unless a form different from the one specified by the Secretary of State is used, and then the fee is $6.00 [§ 9.408(a)]. (See Appendix B for a copy of the approved Financing Statement.) The businessman should remember that, if he wishes, he may file a copy of the security agreement itself, providing it contains the formal requisites and the proper fee is tendered [§ 9.402(a)].

Once properly filed, the perfection continues for sixty (60) days *after* the stated maturity date of the financing statement where the maturity date is of a duration of five (5) years or less. All other financing statements, whether on demand or otherwise, are effective for five (5) years from the date of filing [§ 9.402(b)]. After this period, the security interest becomes unperfected *unless* the secured party files a continuation statement within six (6) months prior to the expiration date to continue the perfected interest. This continuation is good for five (5) years and, upon lapse of this period, can be continued again using the same procedure [§ 9.403(c)]. The fee for the continuation is $3.00. (See Appendix C for approved Continuation Form.)

The following is an example of a situation when the filing of a continuation could be very important. Assume that A on March 1 makes a nonpurchase money advance and files his security interest that same date. On September 1 of that same year, B makes a similar advance on the same collateral and files that same date. At this point, A obviously has priority over B as to the security interest in the collateral. If A does not file a continuation and his interest should lapse before B's, B now has priority over A's unperfected interest.

The secured party of record may, by his signed statement, release all or a part of any collateral described in a filed financing statement, thereby freeing his security interest in that part of the collateral. The filing fee for the release is $3.00 [§ 9.406]. (See Appendix C for an approved Form of Release.)

The secured party may also assign all or part of his security interest to an assignee. The assignee usually wishes to become the secured party of record. If such is done by a disclosure method as provided for under the Code—such as on the front or back of the financing statement—the filing fee is $3.00 [§ 9.405(a)]. If the secured party files a separate written statement of assignment, the filing fee is $3.00 [§ 9.405(b)]. (See Appendix C for approved Form of Assignment.)

The ultimate goal of the parties is to have the debt paid and the security interest terminated. The basic fee for filing such a termination statement is $3.00. Should the secured party fail to file such or furnish the debtor with a termination statement within ten (10) days after proper demand (written) is made of him, the secured party is liable to the debtor for $100 and, in addition, any loss caused by the debtor by such failure. Once the termination statement is presented to the filing officer, he must note it in the index; then he *removes* from the files, *marks* "terminated," and *sends or delivers* to the secured party the financing statement and any continuation statement, statement of assignment, or statement of release pertaining thereto [§ 9.404].

The filing officer must furnish certain information upon request to certain parties. For example, the person filing any of the above statements may furnish the filing officer a duplicate, requesting the officer to note on such copy the file number and date and hour of the filing of the original. The filing officer sends this copy to the person making the request without charge [§ 9.407(a)].

More commonly, other prospective secured parties will request of the filing officer a certificate stating information on possible perfected financing statements with respect to a named debtor. The fee for such a certificate is $5.00; however, if the number of statements reported therein exceeds ten (10), then the fee for the certificate shall be $5.00 plus $1.00 for each statement over ten (10). Also, if requested, the filing officer will furnish a copy of any filed financing statement or assignment at $1.00 *per page copied*, but not less than $5.00 per request concerning a debtor. In light of priorities and the concept of the floating lien, a businessman might well request such information before advancing credit to a particular debtor. (See Appendix D for approved Information Form.)

Microfilming of the above discussed documents is now permitted by county clerks.

RIGHTS AND DUTIES OF THE PARTIES

Generally, a secured party in possession of the collateral must use reasonable care in the custody and preservation of the collateral and is subject to liability by his debtor for his failure to do so, although he does not lose his security interest. He may also use or operate the collateral as permitted in the security agreement, or he may use the collateral to preserve its value. Should the collateral in his possession increase in value or should profits be derived from the collateral, the secured party may hold these increases as additional security *unless* they are in the form of money. Should the increase be in money, unless remitted to the debtor, it shall be applied in reduction of the secured obligation [§ 9.207].

The secured party must keep the collateral identifiable, except, when the collateral is fungible, it may be commingled. He may repledge the collateral, but he must do so upon terms which do not impair the debtor's right to redeem it upon paying the debt [§ 9.207].

Unless the security agreement provides to the contrary, the debtor is responsible for all *reasonable* charges incurred in the custody, preservation, and operation of the collateral in the possession of the secured party. These charges include costs of insurance, taxes, storage, and like costs [§ 9.207].

If the debtor wishes, he may sign a statement indicating what he believes to be the aggregate amount of the unpaid indebtedness as of a specific date and, under certain circumstances, include a list of collateral covered by the security agreement, with the request that the secured party approve or correct the list or statement. The secured party, unless he has a reasonable excuse, must comply with such a request within two weeks of receipt, or he is liable for any loss caused to the debtor by such failure. It is obvious the debtor could be a nuisance by making numerous and continuous requests to harass the secured party. The Code provides that the debtor is entitled to such a request once every six (6) months *without charge*. For each additional request made during this period, the secured party may require payment of a charge not exceeding $10.00 [§ 9.208].

The debtor's obligation is to pay the debt according to the terms of the security agreement. The debtor is in default upon nonpayment *or* upon the happening of any event or condition which materially breaches the security agreement.

REMEDIES UPON DEFAULT

In general, when the debtor is in default, the secured party may reduce his claim to judgment, foreclose, or otherwise enforce the security interest by any available judicial procedure [§ 9.501]. Since these remedies are presently in use, there is no need to go into further explanation here.

Unless otherwise agreed, the secured party has on default the right to take possession of the collateral, and this can be done without judicial process *if* such possession can be obtained without a breach of the peace. The businessman should not attempt to break into the debtor's home or take by force the collateral from an unwilling debtor. He may find not only criminal charges being filed but an action in tort for any damage the debtor may have sustained. In addition, upon default, if the security agreement so provides, the secured party may require the debtor to assemble the collateral and make such available at a certain place reasonably convenient to both. If, for some reason, it is impractical to move the collateral or too expensive to store, the Code gives the secured party the right to render the collateral unusable to the debtor and, upon following the proper procedure, dispose of it on the debtor's premises [§ 9.503].

To illustrate, suppose B, bank, has a security interest in certain oil and gas equipment owned by a debtor located on the debtor's premises, and the debtor is in default. Since it might be exceedingly expensive or perhaps impractical to move or store such equipment, the secured party could render such equipment unusable and could dispose of it on the debtor's premises. The secured party must only exercise this right when such action is reasonable under the circumstances.

Once the secured party obtains possession, he *generally* has the right to sell, lease, or otherwise dispose of the collateral in its then existing condition or following any commercially reasonable preparation or process [§ 9.504(a)].

If the secured party sells the collateral, the sale in all aspects must be done in a "commercially reasonable manner." Although the term "commercially reasonable manner" is not defined in the Code, the businessman who follows the statute and conducts the sale in good faith has usually complied. The Code does provide certain actions as being commercially reasonable. They are as follows [§ 9.507]:

1. The fact that a better price could have been obtained by a sale at a different time or in a different place from that selected by the secured party is not enough in and of itself to constitute an unreasonable commercial sale.

2. If the secured party sells the collateral in the usual manner in any recognized market at the current price, the sale is commercially reasonable.

3. If the secured party sells the collateral in conformity with the reasonable commercial practice among dealers in that type of property, the sale is commercially reasonable.

4. A disposition which has been approved in any judicial proceeding or by any bona fide creditors' committee or representative of creditors shall *conclusively* be deemed to be commercially reasonable.

If the secured party does sell, the collateral may be disposed of at a *public* or *private* sale if done in a commercially reasonable manner. Unless the collateral is perishable or threatens to decline speedily in value or is of a type customarily sold on a recognized market, the secured party *must give* the debtor *reasonable notice* of the time and place of the sale. In addition, except in the case of consumer goods, such notice must also be sent to other secured parties who have filed on the collateral to be sold and any other secured parties that are known by the secured party to have security interests in the collateral. Failure of the secured party to give notice makes him liable for an ensuing loss. The secured party may buy at any public sale, and he is authorized by the Code to buy at a private sale *if* the collateral customarily is sold in a recognized market or is of a type which is the subject of a widely distributed standard price quotation [§ 9.504(c)]. It should be noted here that the Code provides that these provisions as stated in this paragraph may not be waived or varied [§ 9.501(c)(2)].

The proceeds of the sale are applied first to the expenses incurred by the secured party in retaking, holding, and selling the collateral. This would include reasonable attorneys' fees *if* the security agreement so provided. After these expenses have been deducted, the remaining proceeds are applied to the indebtedness of the secured party. If any proceeds are then left, junior security interests, if any, are to be satisfied *if* the junior interest has made a written demand for payment before a distribution of proceeds was made. The secured party may demand that the junior security interest give reasonable proof of his claim [§ 9.504(a)]. Even though a businessman may find his security interest to be second in priority, it is still possible that he may receive a part of the proceeds in satisfaction of his claim, if he will follow the above procedure.

As a general rule, if any surplus is left after the above expenses, indebtedness, and junior security interests have been satisfied, it goes to the debtor [§ 9.504(b)]. The duty to account to the debtor for this surplus cannot be waived or varied by agreement [§ 9.501(c)(1)]. Should the proceeds not cover the expenses and the indebtedness to the secured party, *unless waived*, the debtor is liable for the deficiency. If the collateral involves the sale of accounts, contract rights, or chattel paper, the rules as to the application of surplus and deficiency are applicable only *if* they are so provided for in the security agreement [§ 9.504(b)].

The Code provides that, except in a case where the debtor has paid 60 percent of the obligation in consumer goods, the secured party, upon obtaining possession of the goods of a defaulting debtor, may *retain* the collateral *in satisfaction* of the secured obligation. This collateral can be retained in satisfaction only if the secured party sends written notice of such intention to the debtor and (except in the case of consumer goods) any other secured party who has filed or is known to have a secured interest in the collateral. If no objection is received by these parties within thirty (30) days, the secured party may retain the collateral as provided above. If any objection is received, the collateral must be disposed of as previously discussed [§ 9.505].

In the case of consumer goods where the debtor has paid 60 percent or more of the obligation but is in default, unless he has signed a statement renouncing his rights, the secured party must dispose of the collateral as previously discussed within ninety (90) days after taking possession [§ 9.505(a)]. Should the secured party fail to do so within this period, the debtor may, at his option, recover in an action in conversion [§ 9.505(a)] or recover an amount not less than the credit service charge plus 10 percent of the principal amount of the debt or the time price differential plus 10 percent of the cash price [§ 9.507(a)]. It is obvious that the secured party loses by waiting too long in pursuing a prompt disposal of the collateral in this situation.

The debtor or any other secured party, unless waived in writing *after* default, may redeem the collateral at any time before the secured party has disposed of or entered into a contract for disposition of the collateral. The redemption is accomplished by tendering fulfillment of all obligations secured by the collateral as well as all costs incurred by the secured party [§ 9.506]. A sale or part of the collateral does not remove the right of redemption for any collateral left in the hands of the secured party. The right of redemption cannot be waived in any other manner except as provided above [§ 9.501(c)(4)].

When collateral is disposed of by a secured party after default of the debtor, a purchaser for value receives all of the debtor's rights in the collateral *free* from the security interest and all junior interests and liens. The Code will allow the purchaser to take free, even though the secured party failed to comply with the requirements of disposal under the Code or judicial proceedings, if the purchaser at the sale had no knowledge of such interests or rights and bought in good faith [§ 9.504(d)].

SOLDIERS AND SAILORS CIVIL RELIEF ACT

The remedies afforded a secured party upon the default of the debtor are subject to the security agreement and those provided by law. Realizing that some persons entering the active military services may be handicapped in meeting certain financial and other obligations incurred prior to their entering active service, Congress enacted legislation to grant some relief to their plight. The legislation is a part of the Soldiers and Sailors Civil Relief Act of 1940 as amended.

The act is not a bar to proceed against one in the military service but allows the court to stay any proceedings or remedy which may be used against him when his military obligation materially affects his ability to prosecute, defend, or meet his financial obligations. Under the act, a secured party whose security interest arose prior to the debtor entering the service could not exercise any right or option under the contract to rescind or terminate the contract or resume possession by reason of breach of the debtor except by action of the court, which rarely is given. Thus, the remedies previously discussed usually would be inapplicable as against a debtor who has entered the military service.

The act applies only to financial obligations incurred *prior* to his entrance into the active military service. The protective period, assuming his military service materially affects his ability to meet his financial obligation, begins with receipt of the order of induction and may continue up to six months after his military service is terminated. In addition, the court may extend the time in which the debtor may make payments in such a way as to be fair to both parties.

CONTINUATION AND TERMINATION OF PRECODE SECURITY INTERESTS

Precode security interests eventually would be terminated with the passage of time. The uncertainty of just when such interests would terminate has placed a definite need for the checking of precode records as well as those filed under the Uniform Commercial Code. The Code has been amended to provide that with few exceptions precode interests either have been terminated on July 1, 1971, or, to be continued, have been filed under the Code. Thus, as of July 1, 1971, the records of the Secretary of State and county clerks reflected all recorded interests in the state of Texas, with only a few exceptions.

The law provides that precode security interests dealing with (1) chattel mortgage filings, (2) factors' liens, etc., which require no further filing, (3) security interests perfected precode without filing but which now requires filing under the Code, and (4) all precode filings which require further filing, refiling, or recording, such as accounts receivable or trust receipts, lapsed on the precode lapse date or July 1, 1971, whichever was earlier, *unless* a financing statement is filed prior to the lapse date. This filing will constitute a continuation and not a new perfection for priority purposes. The form of continuation is the same as Appendix C except the debtor need not sign, *and* it must state on the form "Already subject to a precode perfected security interest" [§ 10.102(2)].

Transactions which required filing before the Code, such as a purchase money security interest in consumer goods, continue or are perfected without filing under the Code. If there are any precode unperfected security interests, they may now be perfected by filing or the taking of possession as provided under the Code. After December 31, 1967, no more filings may be made under precode law, *except* a certificate of payment or other satisfaction or discharge [§ 10.102(3)].

APPENDIX A
SECURITY AGREEMENTS

The following forms have been reproduced with the permission of and through the courtesy of Steck-Warlick Company, Austin, Texas.

15-1560 (1554)—SECURITY AGREEMENT—GENERAL—LONG FORM—CLASS 4 THE STECK-WARLICK CO., AUSTIN

SECURITY AGREEMENT

____
Debtor's Name Street Address

____
City County State

(hereinafter called in accordance with the terms and provisions of the Uniform Commercial Code – DEBTOR) for value received hereby grants to ______________________________
Secured Party's Name

(hereinafter called in accordance with the terms and provisions of the Uniform Commercial Code – SECURED PARTY) whose address is ______________________________,
Street City, County, and State

a security interest in and mortgages to SECURED PARTY the following described property (which hereinafter is referred to as COLLATERAL) to-wit:

(Note.— If COLLATERAL is crops, or oil, gas or minerals to be extracted, or timber to be cut, or if COLLATERAL is to become a fixture, describe in the above space following the description of the COLLATERAL the real estate concerned, and give the name of the record owner hereof.)

to secure DEBTOR'S note to SECURED PARTY dated ________________, 19____, for $________________.

DEBTOR warrants and covenants: (Note – Place checkmark (V) or DEBTOR'S initials in the blank space before each statement which applies to this agreement.)

____ COLLATERAL is to be used for personal, family, or household purposes.

____ COLLATERAL is to be used in business other than farming operations.

____ COLLATERAL is equipment used in farming operations, or farm products, or accounts, contract rights or general intangibles arising from or relating to the sale of farm products by a farmer.

____ COLLATERAL is accounts or contract rights and the records concerning same are kept at

____,

or if left blank at address given for DEBTOR.

____ COLLATERAL is a fixture attached to or to become a fixture attached to the above described land.

____ COLLATERAL is being acquired by DEBTOR from SECURED PARTY or is being acquired with the proceeds of the advance evidenced by this agreement.

____ DEBTOR'S residence is at the above address.

____ DEBTOR'S residence is at

____

____ COLLATERAL will be kept at DEBTOR'S residence.

____ COLLATERAL will be kept at

____

____ DEBTOR'S chief place of business is in the county of DEBTOR'S residence.

____ DEBTOR'S chief place of business is at

____

The warranties, covenants, terms and agreements on the reverse side hereof are incorporated herein and made a part hereof for all intents and purposes. DEBTOR and SECURED PARTY as used in this Security Agreement include the heirs, executors or administrators, successors or assigns of those parties.

____

Dated ____ ____

Signature of DEBTOR

DEBTOR WARRANTS, COVENANTS AND AGREES:

1. **Title**—Except for the security interest hereby granted, Debtor has, or upon acquisition will have, full fee simple title to Collateral free from any lien, security interest, encumbrance, or claim, and Debtor will, at Debtor's cost and expense defend any action which may affect Secured Party's security interest in or Debtor's title to Collateral.

2. **Financing Statement**—That no Financing Statement covering Collateral or any part thereof or any proceeds thereof is on file in any public office and at Secured Party's request Debtor will join in executing all necessary Financing Statements in forms satisfactory to Secured Party and will pay the cost of filing same and will further execute all other necessary instruments deemed necessary by Secured Party and pay the cost of filing same.

3. **Sale, lease, or disposition of Collateral**—Debtor will not, without written consent of Secured Party sell, contact to sell, lease, encumber or dispose of Collateral or any interest therein until this Security Agreement and all debts secured thereby have been fully satisfied.

4. **Insurance**—Debtor will insure the Collateral with companies acceptable to Secured Party against such casualties and in such amounts as Secured Party shall require with a standard mortgage clause in favor of Secured Party and Secured Party is hereby authorized to collect sums which may become due under any of said policies and apply same to the obligations hereby secured.

5. **Protection of Collateral**—Debtor will keep the Collateral in good order and repair and will not waste or destroy Collateral or any part thereof. Debtor will not use the Collateral in violation of any statute or ordinance and Secured Party will have the right to examine and inspect Collateral at any reasonable time.

6. **Taxes**—Debtor will pay promptly when due all taxes and assessments upon the Collateral or for its use and operation.

7. **Location and Identification**—Debtor will keep the Collateral separate and identifiable and at the address shown on the front page hereof and will not remove the Collateral from said address without Secured Party's written consent.

8. **Additional Security Interest**—Debtor hereby grants to Secured Party a security interest in and to all proceeds, increases, substitutions, replacements, additions, and accessions to the Collateral. This provision shall not be construed to mean that Debtor is authorized to sell, lease, or dispose of Collateral without Secured Party's consent.

9. **Future Indebtedness**—The security interest hereby granted secures the indebtedness described on the front page hereof and all other obligations of Debtor to Secured Party, direct or indirect, absolute or contingent, due or to become due, whether existing or hereafter arising.

10. **Decrease in Value of Collateral**—Debtor will, if in Secured Party's judgment the Collateral has materially decreased in value or if Secured Party shall at any time deem that Secured Party is insecure, either provide enough additional Collateral to satisfy Secured Party or reduce the total indebtedness by an amount sufficient to satisfy Secured Party.

11. **Re-imbursement of expenses**—At Secured Party's option, Secured Party may discharge taxes, liens, interest, or perform or cause to be performed for and in behalf of Debtor any actions and conditions, obligations or covenants which Debtor has failed or refused to perform and may pay for the repair, maintenance, and preservation of Collateral and all sums so expended, including but not limited to, attorney's fees, court costs, agent's fees, or commissions, or any other costs or expenses shall bear interest from the date of payment at the rate of 10% per annum and shall be payable at the place designated in the above described note and shall be secured by this Security Agreement.

12. **Payment**—Debtor will pay the note secured by this Security Agreement and any renewal or extension thereof and any other indebtedness hereby secured in accordance with the terms and provisions thereof and will repay immediately all sums expended by Secured Party in accordance with the terms and provisions of this Security Agreement.

13. **Change of Residence or Place of Business**—Debtor will promptly notify Secured Party of any change of Debtor's residence, chief place of business or place where records concerning accounts and contract rights are kept.

14. **Attorney-in-Fact**—Debtor hereby appoints Secured Party Debtor's attorney-in-fact to do any and every act which Debtor is obligated by this Security Agreement to do and to exercise all rights of Debtor in Collateral and to make collections and to execute any and all papers and instruments and to do all other things necessary to preserve and protect Collateral and to protect Secured Party's security interest in said Collateral.

15. **Time-Waiver**—Debtor agrees that in performing any act under this Security Agreement and the note secured thereby that time shall be of the essence and that Secured Party's acceptance of partial or delinquent payments, or failure of Secured Party to exercise any right or remedy shall not be a waiver of any obligation of Debtor or right of Secured Party or constitute a waiver of any other similar default subsequently occurring.

16. **Default**—Debtor shall be in default under this Security Agreement upon the happening of any of the following events or conditions:

    1. Default in the payment or performance of any note obligation, covenant or liability contained or referred to herein;
    2. Any warranty, representation or statement made or furnished to Secured Party by or in behalf of Debtor proves to have been false in any material respect when made or furnished;
    3. Any event which results in the acceleration of the maturity of the indebtedness of Debtor to others under any indenture, agreement or undertaking;
    4. Loss, theft, substantial damage, destruction, sale or encumbrance to or of any of the Collateral, or the making of any levy, seizure or attachment thereof or thereon;
    5. Any time the Secured Party believes that the prospect of payment of any indebtedness secured hereby or the performance of this Security Agreement is impaired;
    6. Death, dissolution, termination of existence, insolvency, business failure, appointment of a receiver for any part of the Collateral assignment for the benefit of creditors or the commencement of any proceeding under any bankruptcy or insolvency law by or against Debtor or any guarantor or surety for Debtor.

17. **Remedies**—Upon the occurrence of any such event of default, and at any time thereafter, Secured Party may declare all obligations secured hereby immediately due and payable and may proceed to enforce payment of the same and exercise any and all of the rights and remedies provided by the Uniform Commercial Code as well as all other rights and remedies possessed by Secured Party. Secured Party may require Debtor to assemble the Collateral and make it available to Secured Party at any place to be designated by Secured Party which is reasonably convenient to both parties. Unless the Collateral is perishable or threatens to decline speedily in value or is of a type customarily sold on a recognized market, Secured Party will give Debtor reasonable notice of the time and place of any public sale thereof or of the time after which any private sale or any other intended disposition thereof is to be made. The requirements of reasonable notice shall be met if such notice is mailed, postage prepaid, to the address of Debtor shown at the beginning of this Security Agreement at least five days before the time of the sale or disposition. Expenses of retaking, holding, preparing for sale, selling or the like shall include Secured Party's reasonable attorney's fees and legal expenses.

FORM NO. 1561—SECURITY AGREEMENT—GENERAL—AND NOTE—CLASS 4 THE STECK CO., AUSTIN

SECURITY AGREEMENT AND COMBINED NOTE

____
(Debtor's Name) Street Address

____
City County State

(hereinafter called in accordance with the terms and provisions of the Uniform Commercial Code—DEBTOR) for value received promises to pay to the order of

____
(Secured Party's Name)

(hereinafter called in accordance with the terms and provisions of the Uniform Commercial Code—SECURED PARTY) whose address is

____
Street Address City, County, and State

at ____

the sum of $______________, with interest thereon at the rate of ________% per annum, interest payable ______________________. This combined note and security agreement is payable as follows:

Failure upon the part of DEBTOR to pay the principal or interest of this combined note and security agreement as the same accrues or failure to perform any of the terms, provisions and obligations of this combined note and security agreement shall entitle Secured Party to declare the entire sum unpaid thereon immediately due and payable. All past due principal and interest shall bear interest at the rate of 10% per annum.

DEBTOR and any endorsers hereof severally waive presentment of payment, notice of non-payment, protest and notice of protest, and diligence in collection.

To secure the payment of this combined note and security agreement and all obligations of DEBTOR hereunder, DEBTOR hereby grants to SECURED PARTY a security interest in and mortgages to SECURED PARTY the following described property (hereinafter referred to as COLLATERAL) to-wit:

(Note — If COLLATERAL is crops, or oil, gas or minerals to be extracted, or timber to be cut, or if COLLATERAL is to become a fixture, describe in the above space following the description of the COLLATERAL the real estate concerned, and give the name of the record owner thereof.)

DEBTOR warrants and covenants: (Note—Place checkmark (V) or DEBTOR'S initials in the blank space before each statement which applies to this agreement.)

_____ COLLATERAL is to be used for personal, family, or household purposes.

_____ COLLATERAL is to be used in business other than farming operations.

_____ COLLATERAL is equipment used in farming operations, or farm products, or accounts, contract rights or general intangibles arising from or relating to the sale of farm products by a farmer.

_____ COLLATERAL is accounts or contract rights and the records concerning same are kept at

______________________________________,
or if left blank at address given for DEBTOR.

_____ COLLATERAL is a fixture attached to or to become a fixture attached to the above described land.

_____ COLLATERAL is being acquired by DEBTOR from SECURED PARTY or is being acquired with the proceeds of the advance evidenced by this agreement.

_____ DEBTOR'S residence is at the above address.

_____ DEBTOR'S residence is at

____

_____ COLLATERAL will be kept at DEBTOR'S residence.

_____ COLLATERAL will be kept at

____

_____ DEBTOR'S chief place of business is in the county of DEBTOR'S residence.

_____ DEBTOR'S chief place of business is at

____

The warranties, covenants, terms and agreements on the reverse side hereof are incorporated herein and made a part hereof for all intents and purposes. DEBTOR and SECURED PARTY as used in this Security Agreement include the heirs, executors or administrators, successors or assigns of those parties.

____

Dated ______________________________ ______________________________________

Signature of DEBTOR

DEBTOR WARRANTS, COVENANTS AND AGREES:

1. **Title**—Except for the security interest hereby granted, Debtor has, or upon acquisition will have, full fee simple title to Collateral free from any lien, security interest, encumbrance, or claim, and Debtor will, at Debtor's cost and expense defend any action which may affect Secured Party's security interest in or Debtor's title to Collateral.

2. **Financing Statement**—That no Financing Statement covering Collateral or any part thereof or any proceeds thereof is on file in any public office and at Secured Party's request Debtor will join in executing all necessary Financing Statements in forms satisfactory to Secured Party and will pay the cost of filing same and will further execute all other necessary instruments deemed necessary by Secured Party and pay the cost of filing same.

3. **Sale, lease, or disposition of Collateral**—Debtor will not, without written consent of Secured Party sell, contact to sell, lease, encumber or dispose of Collateral or any interest therein until this Security Agreement and all debts secured thereby have been fully satisfied.

4. **Insurance**—Debtor will insure the Collateral with companies acceptable to Secured Party against such casualties and in such amounts as Secured Party shall require with a standard mortgage clause in favor of Secured Party and Secured Party is hereby authorized to collect sums which may become due under any of said policies and apply same to the obligations hereby secured.

5. **Protection of Collateral**—Debtor will keep the Collateral in good order and repair and will not waste or destroy Collateral or any part thereof. Debtor will not use the Collateral in violation of any statute or ordinance and Secured Party will have the right to examine and inspect Collateral at any reasonable time.

6. **Taxes**—Debtor will pay promptly when due all taxes and assessments upon the Collateral or for its use and operation.

7. **Location and Identification**—Debtor will keep the Collateral separate and identifiable and at the address shown on the front page hereof and will not remove the Collateral from said address without Secured Party's written consent.

8. **Additional Security Interest**—Debtor hereby grants to Secured Party a security interest in and to all proceeds, increases, substitutions, replacements, additions, and accessions to the Collateral. This provision shall not be construed to mean that Debtor is authorized to sell, lease, or dispose of Collateral without Secured Party's consent.

9. **Future Indebtedness**—The security interest hereby granted secures the indebtedness described on the front page hereof and all other obligations of Debtor to Secured Party, direct or indirect, absolute or contingent, due or to become due, whether existing or hereafter arising.

10. **Decrease in Value of Collateral**—Debtor will, if in Secured Party's judgment the Collateral has materially decreased in value or if Secured Party shall at any time deem that Secured Party is insecure, either provide enough additional Collateral to satisfy Secured Party or reduce the total indebtedness by an amount sufficient to satisfy Secured Party.

11. **Re-imbursement of expenses**—At Secured Party's option, Secured Party may discharge taxes, liens, interest, or perform or cause to be performed for and in behalf of Debtor any actions and conditions, obligations or covenants which Debtor has failed or refused to perform and may pay for the repair, maintenance, and preservation of Collateral and all sums so expended, including but not limited to, attorney's fees, court costs, agent's fees, or commissions, or any other costs or expenses shall bear interest from the date of payment at the rate of 10% per annum and shall be payable at the place designated in the above described note and shall be secured by this Security Agreement.

12. **Payment**—Debtor will pay the note secured by this Security Agreement and any renewal or extension thereof and any other indebtedness hereby secured in accordance with the terms and provisions thereof and will repay immediately all sums expended by Secured Party in accordance with the terms and provisions of this Security Agreement.

13. **Change of Residence or Place of Business**—Debtor will promptly notify Secured Party of any change of Debtor's residence, chief place of business or place where records concerning accounts and contract rights are kept.

14. **Attorney-in-Fact**—Debtor hereby appoints Secured Party Debtor's attorney-in-fact to do any and every act which Debtor is obligated by this Security Agreement to do and to exercise all rights of Debtor in Collateral and to make collections and to execute any and all papers and instruments and to do all other things necessary to preserve and protect Collateral and to protect Secured Party's security interest in said Collateral.

15. **Time-Waiver**—Debtor agrees that in performing any act under this Security Agreement and the note secured thereby that time shall be of the essence and that Secured Party's acceptance of partial or delinquent payments, or failure of Secured Party to exercise any right or remedy shall not be a waiver of any obligation of Debtor or right of Secured Party or constitute a waiver of any other similar default subsequently occurring.

16. **Default**—Debtor shall be in default under this Security Agreement upon the happening of any of the following events or conditions:

    1. Default in the payment or performance of any note obligation, covenant or liability contained or referred to herein;
    2. Any warranty, representation or statement made or furnished to Secured Party by or in behalf of Debtor proves to have been false in any material respect when made or furnished;
    3. Any event which results in the acceleration of the maturity of the indebtedness of Debtor to others under any indenture, agreement or undertaking;
    4. Loss, theft, substantial damage, destruction, sale or encumbrance to or of any of the Collateral, or the making of any levy, seizure or attachment thereof or thereon;
    5. Any time the Secured Party believes that the prospect of payment of any indebtedness secured hereby or the performance of this Security Agreement is impaired;
    6. Death, dissolution, termination of existence, insolvency, business failure, appointment of a receiver for any part of the Collateral assignment for the benefit of creditors or the commencement of any proceeding under any bankruptcy or insolvency law by or against Debtor or any guarantor or surety for Debtor.

17. **Remedies**—Upon the occurrence of any such event of default, and at any time thereafter, Secured Party may declare all obligations secured hereby immediately due and payable and may proceed to enforce payment of the same and exercise any and all of the rights and remedies provided by the Uniform Commercial Code as well as all other rights and remedies possessed by Secured Party. Secured Party may require Debtor to assemble the Collateral and make it available to Secured Party at any place to be designated by Secured Party which is reasonably convenient to both parties. Unless the Collateral is perishable or threatens to decline speedily in value or is of a type customarily sold on a recognized market, Secured Party will give Debtor reasonable notice of the time and place of any public sale thereof or of the time after which any private sale or any other intended disposition thereof is to be made. The requirements of reasonable notice shall be met if such notice is mailed, postage prepaid, to the address of Debtor shown at the beginning of this Security Agreement at least five days before the time of the sale or disposition. Expenses of retaking, holding, preparing for sale, selling or the like shall include Secured Party's reasonable attorney's fees and legal expenses.

FORM NO. 1558—SECURITY AGREEMENT—CLASS 4

THE STECK CO., AUSTIN

SECURITY AGREEMENT
(INVENTORY)

____

Debtor's Name   Street Address

____

City   County   State

(hereinafter called in accordance with the terms and provisions of the Uniform Commercial Code – DEBTOR) for value received hereby grants to ____

Secured Party's Name

(hereinafter called in accordance with the terms and provisions of the Uniform Commercial Code – SECURED PARTY) whose address is ____

Street   City, County, and State

a security interest in the following described inventory of DEBTOR, to-wit:

and all DEBTOR'S inventory of like kinds of types whenever acquired, by way of replacement, substitution, addition or otherwise and all accessions thereto and all proceeds of its sale and all contract rights with respect thereto, all of which is hereafter called INVENTORY. The security interest hereby granted secures the payment of a note in the original principal sum of $_______________, of even date herewith executed by DEBTOR and payable to SECURED PARTY and bearing interest and payable as provided therein. This security interest also secures any and all other loans which SECURED PARTY may at SECURED PARTY'S discretion be willing to make to DEBTOR and shall also secure any and all other obligations of DEBTOR to SECURED PARTY of every kind and description, direct or indirect, absolute or contingent, due or to become due, now existing or hereafter arising and all of which are hereinafter called OBLIGATIONS.

DEBTOR represents and warrants as follows:

1. INVENTORY is now located and shall be kept at the following locations:

____

Street No.   City, County, and State

Street No. ______________________ City, County, and State

Or if left blank at the address given for DEBTOR above.

2. If any part of INVENTORY is leased or held for lease to customers of DEBTOR and is of a type normally used in more than one state (such as automobile equipment, rolling stock, road building equipment and the like) and DEBTOR has a place of business in more than one state. DEBTOR'S chief place of business is

Street No. ______________________ City, County, and State

Or if left blank at the address given for DEBTOR above.

3. If Debtor has an office in more than one state, the office where Debtor keeps the records concerning accounts and contract rights is

Street No. ______________________ City, County, and State

Or if left blank at the address given for DEBTOR above.

4. DEBTOR shall from time to time, as requested by SECURED PARTY, deliver to SECURED PARTY detail descriptions and lists of INVENTORY showing the reasonable fair market value of each item so described and also deliver such other reports and information as reasonably necessary for SECURED PARTY to determine value of INVENTORY. DEBTOR and SECURED PARTY as used in this Security Agreement include the heirs, executors or administrators, successors or assigns of those parties.

The warranties, covenants, terms and agreements on the reverse side hereof are incorporated herein and made a part hereof for all intents and purposes.

Dated ______________________

______________________ ______________________

Signature of SECURED PARTY ______________________ Signature of DEBTOR

DEBTOR WARRANTS, COVENANTS:

Title—Except for the security interest hereby granted, Debtor has, or upon acquisition will have, full fee simple title to Inventory free from any lien, security interest, encumbrance, or claim, and Debtor will, at Debtor's cost and expense defend any action which may affect Secured Party's security interest in or Debtor's title to Inventory.

Financing Statement—That no Financing Statement covering Inventory or any part thereof or any proceeds thereof is on file in any public office and at Secured Party's request Debtor will join in executing all necessary Financing Statements in forms satisfactory to Secured Party and will pay the cost of filing same and will further execute all other necessary instruments deemed necessary by Secured Party and pay the cost of filing same.

Protection of Inventory—Debtor will keep the Inventory in good order and repair and will not waste or destroy Inventory or any part thereof. Debtor will not use the Inventory in violation of any statute or ordinance and Secured Party will have the right to examine and inspect Inventory at any reasonable time.

Taxes—Debtor will pay promptly when due all taxes and assessments upon the Inventory or for its use and operation.

Insurance—Debtor will insure the Inventory with companies acceptable to Secured Party against such casualties and in such amounts as Secured Party shall require with standard mortgage clause in favor of Secured Party and Secured Party is hereby authorized to collect all sums which may become due under any of said policies and apply same to the obligations hereby secured.

Places of Business—Debtor will promptly notify Secured Party in writing of any addition to, change in or discontinuance of address of Debtor, place or places where inventory is kept, Debtor's chief place of business and/or location of office where records concerning accounts and contract rights are kept.

Decrease in Value of Inventory—Debtor will, if in Secured Party's judgment the Inventory has materially decreased in value or if Secured Party shall at any time deem that Secured Party is insecure, either provide enough additional Inventory to satisfy Secured Party or reduce the total indebtedness by an amount sufficient to satisfy Secured Party.

Re-imbursement of Expenses—At Secured Party's option, Secured Party may discharge taxes, liens, interest, or perform or cause to be performed for and in behalf of Debtor any actions and conditions, obligations or covenants which Debtor has failed or refused to perform and may pay for the repair, maintenance and preservation of Inventory and all sums so expended, including but not limited to, attorney's fees, court costs, agent's fees, or commissions, or any other costs or expenses shall bear interest from the date of payment at the rate of 10% per annum and shall be payable at the place designated in the above described note and shall be secured by this Security Agreement.

Payment—Debtor will pay the note secured by this Security Agreement and any renewal or extension thereof and any other indebtedness hereby secured in accordance with the terms and provisions thereof and will repay immediately all sums expended by Secured Party in accordance with the terms and provisions of this Security Agreement.

Attorney-in-Fact—Debtor hereby appoints Secured Party Debtor's attorney-in-fact to do any and every act which Debtor is obligated by this Security Agreement to do and to exercise all rights of Debtor in Inventory and to make collections and to execute any and all papers and instruments and to do all other things necessary to preserve and protect Inventory and to protect Secured Party's security interest in said Inventory.

Time-Waiver—Debtor agrees that in performing any act under this Security Agreement and the note secured thereby that time shall be of the essence and that Secured Party's acceptance of partial or delinquent payments, or failure of Secured Party to exercise any right or remedy shall not be a waiver of any obligation of Debtor or right of Secured Party or constitute a waiver of any other similar default subsequently occurring.

Default—Debtor shall be in default under this Security Agreement upon the happening of any of the following events or conditions:

1. Default in the payment or performance of any note obligation, covenant, or liability contained or referred to herein;
2. Any warranty, representation or statement made or furnished to Secured Party by or in behalf of Debtor proves to have been false in any material respect when made or furnished;
3. Any event which results in the acceleration of the maturity of the indebtedness of Debtor to others under any indenture, agreement or undertaking;
4. Loss, theft, substantial damage, destruction, sale or encumbrance to or of any of the Inventory, or the making of any levy, seizure or attachment thereof or thereon;
5. Any time the Secured Party believes that the prospect of payment of any indebtedness secured hereby or the performance of this Security Agreement is impaired;
6. Death, dissolution, termination of existence, insolvency, business failure, appointment of a receiver for any part of the Inventory assignment for the benefit of creditors or the commencement of any proceeding under any bankruptcy or insolvency law by or against Debtor or any guarantor or surety for Debtor.

Remedies—Upon the occurrence of any such event of default, and at any time thereafter, Secured Party may declare all obligations secured hereby immediately due and payable and may proceed to enforce payment of the same and exercise any and all of the rights and remedies provided by the Uniform Commercial Code as well as all other rights and remedies possessed by Secured Party. Secured Party may require Debtor to assemble the Inventory and make it available to Secured Party at any place to be designated by Secured Party which is reasonably convenient to both parties. Unless the Inventory is perishable or threatens to decline speedily in value or is of a type customarily sold on a recognized market, Secured Party will give Debtor reasonable notice of the time and place of any public sale thereof or of the time after which any private sale or any other intended disposition thereof is to be made. The requirements of reasonable notice shall be met if such notice is mailed, postage prepaid, to the address of Debtor shown at the beginning of this Security Agreement at least five days before the time of the sale or disposition. Expenses of retaking, holding, preparing for sale, selling or the like shall include Secured Party's reasonable attorney's fees and legal expenses.

15-1584(1557) - SECURITY AGREEMENT - EQUIPMENT - CLASS 4 THE STECK-WARLICK CO., AUSTIN

SECURITY AGREEMENT (EQUIPMENT)

____
Debtor's Name Street Address

____
City County State

(hereinafter called in accordance with the terms and provisions of the Uniform Commercial Code – DEBTOR) for value received hereby grants to ________________________________
Secured Party's Name

(hereinafter called in accordance with the terms and provisions of the Uniform Commercial Code – SECURED PARTY) whose address is ________________________________,
Street City, County, and State

a security interest in the following described equipment of DEBTOR (said equipment is hereinafter referred to as COLLATERAL) to-wit:

The security interest hereby granted secures the payment of a note in the original principal sum of $________________, of even date herewith executed by DEBTOR and payable to SECURED PARTY and bearing interest and payable as provided therein.

DEBTOR represents and warrants as follows:

1. Collateral is now located and shall be kept at the following location,

____
Street No. City, County and State

or if left blank at the address given for DEBTOR above.

2. If any part of Collateral is of a type which is normally used in more than one state (such as automobile equipment, rolling stock, airplanes, road building equipment, commercial harvesting equipment, construction machinery, and the like) and DEBTOR has place of business in more than one state, DEBTOR'S chief place of business is

____
Street No. City, County and State

or if left blank at the address given for DEBTOR above.

3. If Collateral has been attached or is to be attached to real property, a description of the real property is as follows: ______________________________

4. DEBTOR'S residence is ______________________________,
Street No. City, County and State

or if left blank at the address given for DEBTOR above.

5. Collateral is to be used for: ☐ farming operation; or ☐ business other than farming operations.

Collateral is ☐ now owned by DEBTOR or ☐ is being acquired by DEBTOR from SECURED PARTY or is being acquired with the proceeds of the advance evidenced by this agreement.

DEBTOR and SECURED PARTY as used in this Security Agreement include the heirs, executors and administrators, successors or assigns of those parties.

The warranties, covenants, terms and agreements on the reverse side hereof are incorporated herein and made a part hereof for all intents and purposes.

____

Dated ______________________ ______________________________
Signature of DEBTOR

DEBTOR WARRANTS, COVENANTS AND AGREES:

Title—Except for the security interest hereby granted, Debtor has, or upon acquisition will have, full fee simple title to Collateral free from any lien, security interest, encumbrance, or claim, and Debtor will, at Debtor's cost and expense defend any action which may affect Secured Party's security interest in or Debtor's title to Collateral.

Financing Statement—That no Financing Statement covering Collateral or any part thereof or any proceeds thereof is on file in any public office and at Secured Party's request Debtor will join in executing all necessary Financing Statements in forms satisfactory to Secured Party and will pay the cost of filing same and will further execute all other necessary instruments deemed necessary by Secured Party and pay the cost of filing same.

Sale, lease, or disposition of Collateral—Debtor will not, without written consent of Secured Party sell, contract to sell, lease, encumber or dispose of Collateral or any interest therein until this Security agreement and all debts secured thereby have been fully satisfied.

Insurance—Debtor will insure the Collateral with companies acceptable to Secured Party against such casualties and in such amounts as Secured Party shall require with a standard mortgage clause in favor of Secured Party and Secured Party is hereby authorized to collect sums which may become due under any of said policies and apply same to the obligations hereby secured.

Protection of Collateral—Debtor will keep the Collateral in good order and repair and will not waste or destroy Collateral or any part thereof. Debtor will not use the Collateral in violation of any statute or ordinance and Secured Party will have the right to examine and inspect Collateral at any reasonable time.

Taxes—Debtor will pay promptly when due all taxes and assessments upon the Collateral or for its use and operation.

Location and Identification—Debtor will keep the Collateral separate and identifiable and at the address shown on the front page hereof and will not remove the Collateral from said address without Secured Party's written consent.

Additional Security Interest—Debtor hereby grants to Secured Party a security interest in and to all proceeds, increases, substitutions, replacements, additions, and accessions to the Collateral, but this provision shall not be construed to mean that Debtor is authorized to sell, lease, or dispose of Collateral without Secured Party's consent.

Change of Residence or Place of Business—Debtor will promptly notify Secured Party in writing of any addition to, change in, or discontinuance of the place where Collateral is to be kept, or Debtor's chief place of business or Debtor's residence.

Future Indebtedness—The security interest hereby granted secures the indebtedness described on the front page hereof and all other obligations of Debtor to Secured Party, direct or indirect, absolute or contingent, due or to become due, whether existing or hereafter arising.

Decrease in Value of Collateral—Debtor will, if in Secured Party's judgment the Collateral has materially decreased in value or if Secured Party shall at any time deem that Secured Party is insecure, either provide enough additional Collateral to satisfy Secured Party or reduce the total indebtedness by an amount sufficient to satisfy Secured Party.

Re-imbursement of expenses—At Secured Party's option, Secured Party may discharge taxes, liens, interest, or perform or cause to be performed for and in behalf of Debtor any actions and conditions, obligations or covenants which Debtor has failed or refused to perform and may pay for the repair, maintenance, and preservation of Collateral and all sums so expended, including but not limited to, attorney's fees, court costs, agent's fees, or commissions, or any other costs or expenses shall bear interest from the date of payment at the rate of 10% per annum and shall be payable at the place designated in the above described note and shall be secured by this Security Agreement.

Payment—Debtor will pay the note secured by this Security Agreement and any renewal or extension thereof and any other indebtedness hereby secured in accordance with the terms and provisions thereof and will repay immediately all sums expended by Secured Party in accordance with the terms and provisions of this Security Agreement.

Attorney-in-Fact—Debtor hereby appoints Secured Party Debtor's attorney-in-fact to do any and every act which Debtor is obligated by this Security Agreement to do and to exercise all rights of Debtor in Collateral and to make collections and to execute any and all papers and instruments and to do all other things necessary to preserve and protect Collateral and to protect Secured Party's security interest in said Collateral.

Time-Waiver—Debtor agrees that in performing any act under this Security Agreement and the note secured thereby that time shall be of the essence and that Secured Party's acceptance of partial or delinquent payments, or failure of Secured Party to exercise any right or remedy shall not be a waiver of any obligation of Debtor or right of Secured Party or constitute a waiver of any other similar default subsequently occurring.

Default—Debtor shall be in default under this Security Agreement upon the happening of any of the following events or conditions:

1. Default in the payment or performance of any obligation, covenant or liability contained or referred to herein;
2. Any warranty, representation or statement made or furnished to Secured Party by or in behalf of Debtor proves to have been false in any material respect when made or furnished;
3. Any event which results in the acceleration of the maturity of the indebtedness of Debtor to others under any indenture, agreement or undertaking;
4. Loss, theft, substantial damage, destruction, sale or encumbrance to or of any of the Collateral, or the making of any levy, seizure or attachment thereof or thereon;
5. Any time the Secured Party believes that the prospect of payment of any indebtedness secured hereby or the performance of this Security Agreement is impaired;
6. Death, dissolution, termination of existence, insolvency, business failure, appointment of a receiver for any part of the Collateral assignment for the benefit of creditors or the commencement of any proceeding under any bankruptcy or insolvency law by or against Debtor or any guarantor or surety for Debtor.

Remedies—Upon the occurrence of any such event of default, and at any time thereafter, Secured Party may declare all obligations secured hereby immediately due and payable and may proceed to enforce payment of the same and exercise any and all of the rights and remedies provided by the Uniform Commercial Code as well as all other rights and remedies possessed by Secured Party. Secured Party may require Debtor to assemble the Collateral and make it available to Secured Party at any place to be designated by Secured Party which is reasonably convenient to both parties. Unless the Collateral is perishable or threatens to decline speedily in value or is of a type customarily sold on a recognized market, Secured Party will give Debtor reasonable notice of the time and place of any public sale thereof or of the time after which any private sale or any other intended disposition thereof is to be made. The requirements of reasonable notice shall be met if such notice is mailed, postage prepaid, to the address of Debtor shown at the beginning of this Security Agreement at least five days before the time of the sale or disposition. Expenses of retaking, holding, preparing for sale, selling or the like shall include Secured Party's reasonable attorney's fees and legal expenses.

FORM NO. 1560—SECURITY AGREEMENT—FARM PRODUCTS—CLASS 4 THE STECK CO., AUSTIN

SECURITY AGREEMENT
(Farm Products)

____
Debtor's Name Street Address

____
City County State

(hereinafter called in accordance with the terms and provisions of the Uniform Commercial Code – DEBTOR) for value received hereby grants to _______________________________
Secured Party's Name

(hereinafter called in accordance with the terms and provisions of the Uniform Commercial Code – SECURED PARTY) whose address is _______________________________,
Street City, County, and State

a security interest in and mortgages to SECURED PARTY the following described FARM PRODUCTS (crops or livestock or supplies used or produced in farming operations or products of crops or livestock in their unmanufactured states), to-wit:

and all young, products and produce thereof and all feed, seed, fertilizer and other supplies now owned or hereafter acquired in connection therewith, all of which hereafter is referred to as COLLATERAL.

to secure DEBTOR'S note to SECURED PARTY dated ____________________, 19____, for $____________________.

DEBTOR represents and warrants as follows:

1. That Debtor is engaged in farming operations and that Collateral is to be used by Debtor in farming operations.

2. That Collateral is located or will be located at ____________________

____,
(Give description of land including county of location)

which land belongs to ____.

3. Debtor's residence is at ____,
Street No. City, County, and State

or if left blank at the address given for Debtor above.

DEBTOR and SECURED PARTY as used in this Security Agreement include the heirs, executors and administrators, successors or assigns of those parties.

The warranties, covenants, terms and agreements on the reverse side hereof are incorporated herein and made a part hereof for all intents and purposes.

Dated ______________________________

______________________________ ______________________________

______________________________ ______________________________
Signature of SECURED PARTY Signature of DEBTOR

DEBTOR WARRANTS, COVENANTS AND AGREES:

Title—Except for the security interest hereby granted, Debtor has, or upon acquisition will have, full fee simple title to Collateral free from any lien, security interest, encumbrance, or claim, and Debtor will, at Debtor's cost and expense defend any action which may affect Secured Party's security interest in or Debtor's title to Collateral.

Financing Statement—That no Financing Statement covering Collateral or any part thereof or any proceeds thereof is on file in any public office and at Secured Party's request Debtor will join in executing all necessary Financing Statements in forms satisfactory to Secured Party and will pay the cost of filing same and will further execute all other necessary instruments deemed necessary by Secured Party and pay the cost of filing same.

Sale, lease, or disposition of Collateral—Debtor will not, without written consent of Secured Party sell, contact to sell, lease, encumber or dispose of Collateral or any interest therein until this Security Agreement and all debts secured thereby have been fully satisfied.

Insurance—Debtor will insure the Collateral with companies acceptable to Secured Party against such casualties and in such amounts as Secured Party shall require with a standard mortgage clause in favor of Secured Party and Secured Party is hereby authorized to collect sums which may become due under any of said policies and apply same to the obligations hereby secured.

Protection of Collateral—Debtor will keep the Collateral in good order and repair and will not waste or destroy Collateral or any part thereof. Debtor will not use the Collateral in violation of any statute or ordinance and Secured Party will have the right to examine and inspect Collateral at any reasonable time.

Taxes—Debtor will pay promptly when due all taxes and assessments upon the Collateral or for its use and operation.

Location and Identification—Debtor will keep the Collateral separate and identifiable and at the address shown on the front page hereof and will not remove the Collateral from said address without Secured Party's written consent.

Additional Security Interest—Debtor hereby grants to Secured Party a security interest in and to all proceeds, increases, substitutions, replacements, additions, and accessions to the Collateral; but this provision shall not be construed to mean that Debtor is authorized to sell, lease, or dispose of Collateral without Secured Party's consent.

Change of Residence—Debtor will promptly notify Secured Party in writing of any change of Debtor's residence.

Future Indebtedness—The security interest hereby granted secures the indebtedness described on the front page hereof and all other obligations of Debtor to Secured Party, direct or indirect, absolute or contingent, due or to become due, whether existing or hereafter arising. That the secured interest hereby granted shall attach to all crops, which become such within three years after this Security Agreement is executed.

Decrease in Value of Collateral—Debtor will, if in Secured Party's judgment the Collateral has materially decreased in value or if Secured Party shall at any time deem that Secured Party is insecure, either provide enough additional Collateral to satisfy Secured Party or reduce the total indebtedness by an amount sufficient to satisfy Secured Party.

Re-imbursement of expenses—At Secured Party's option, Secured Party may discharge taxes, liens, interest, or perform or cause to be performed for and in behalf of Debtor any actions and conditions, obligations or covenants which Debtor has failed or refused to perform and may pay for the repair, maintenance, and preservation of Collateral and all sums so expended, including but not limited to, attorney's fees, court costs, agent's fees, or commissions, or any other costs or expenses shall bear interest from the date of payment at the rate of 10% per annum and shall be payable at the place designated in the above described note and shall be secured by this Security Agreement.

Payment—Debtor will pay the note secured by this Security Agreement and any renewal or extension thereof and any other indebtedness hereby secured in accordance with the terms and provisions thereof and will repay immediately all sums expended by Secured Party in accordance with the terms and provisions of this Security Agreement.

Attorney-in-Fact—Debtor hereby appoints Secured Party Debtor's attorney-in-fact to do any and every act which Debtor is obligated by this Security Agreement to do and to exercise all rights of Debtor in Collateral and to make collections and to execute any and all papers and instruments and to do all other things necessary to preserve and protect Collateral and to protect Secured Party's security interest in said Collateral.

Time-Waiver—Debtor agrees that in performing any act under this Security Agreement and the note secured thereby that time shall be of the essence and that Secured Party's acceptance of partial or delinquent payments, or failure of Secured Party to exercise any right or remedy shall not be a waiver of any obligation of Debtor or right of Secured Party or constitute a waiver of any other similar default subsequently occurring.

Default—Debtor shall be in default under this Security Agreement upon the happening of any of the following events or conditions:

1. Default in the payment or performance of any note, obligation, covenant or liability contained or referred to herein;
2. Any warranty, representation or statement made or furnished to Secured Party by or in behalf of Debtor proves to have been false in any material respect when made or furnished;
3. Any event which results in the acceleration of the maturity of the indebtedness of Debtor to others under any indenture, agreement or undertaking;
4. Loss, theft, substantial damage, destruction, sale or encumbrance to or of any of the Collateral, or the making of any levy, seizure or attachment thereof or thereon;
5. Any time the Secured Party believes that the prospect of payment of any indebtedness secured hereby or the performance of this Security Agreement is impaired;
6. Death, dissolution, termination of existence, insolvency, business failure, appointment of a receiver for any part of the Collateral assignment for the benefit of creditors or the commencement of any proceeding under any bankruptcy or insolvency law by or against Debtor or any guarantor or surety for Debtor.

Remedies—Upon the occurrence of any such event of default, and at any time thereafter, Secured Party may declare all obligations secured hereby immediately due and payable and may proceed to enforce payment of the same and exercise any and all of the rights and remedies provided by the Uniform Commercial Code as well as all other rights and remedies possessed by Secured Party. Secured Party may require Debtor to assemble the Collateral and make it available to Secured Party at any place to be designated by Secured Party which is reasonably convenient to both parties. Unless the Collateral is perishable or threatens to decline speedily in value or is of a type customarily sold on a recognized market, Secured Party will give Debtor reasonable notice of the time and place of any public sale thereof or of the time after which any private sale or any other intended disposition thereof is to be made. The requirements of reasonable notice shall be met if such notice is mailed, postage prepaid, to the address of Debtor shown at the beginning of this Security Agreement at least five days before the time of the sale or disposition. Expenses of retaking, holding, preparing for sale, selling or the like shall include Secured Party's reasonable attorney's fees and legal expenses.

APPENDIX B
FINANCING STATEMENT

The following forms have been reproduced with the permission of and through the courtesy of Steck-Warlick Company, Austin, Texas.

46

Uniform Commercial Code—FINANCING STATEMENT—Form UCC-1 (Rev. 9-71)

"LITHO-SNAP" • • • LITHOGRAPHED BY STECK-WARLICK CO., AUSTIN, TEXAS • • •

IMPORTANT—Read instructions on back before filling out form

This Financing Statement is presented to a Filing Officer for filing pursuant to the Uniform Commercial Code

3. Maturity Date (if any):

1. Debtor(s) (Last name first) and Mailing Address:

2. Secured Party(ies) Name and Address:

4. For Filing Officer (Date, Time, Number and Filing Office):

5. This Financing Statement covers the following types (or items) of collateral. (WARNING: If collateral is crops or fixtures, read instructions on back.)

6. Name and Address of Assignee of Secured Party: (Use this space to describe collateral, if needed)

Check ☒ if covered: ☐ Proceeds of collateral are also covered. ☐ Products of collateral are also covered. Number of additional sheets presented ____

7. This Statement is filed without the Debtor's signature to perfect a security interest in collateral
(Please check appropriate box)
- ☐ already subject to a security interest in another jurisdiction when it was brought into this state, or
- ☐ which is proceeds of the original collateral described above in which a security interest was perfected, or
- ☐ already subject to a financing statement filed in another county, or
- ☐ already subject to a pre-code perfected security interest.

______________________________ ______________________________

By ______________________________
Signature(s) of Debtor(s)

By ______________________________
Signature(s) of Secured Party(ies)

(1) Filing Officer Copy—Numerical

STANDARD FORM—FORM UCC-1 (REV. 9-71) APPROVED BY THE SECRETARY OF STATE OF TEXAS—FORM 15-1548—THE STECK-WARLICK CO., AUSTIN, TEXAS

INSTRUCTIONS

1. PLEASE TYPE this form. Do not write in Box 4. The completion of Box 3 is optional.

2. If collateral is CROPS growing or to be grown, describe real estate concerned and give name of record owner of the realty.

3. If collateral is or will become FIXTURES, describe real estate concerned and give name of record owner of the realty. Also, write in the phrase, "Collateral is or includes fixtures." A financing statement covering fixtures cannot perfect a security interest in non-fixtures. If the collateral includes both fixtures and non-fixtures, separate financing statements for the fixtures and for the non-fixtures must be filed.

4. If the space provided for any item on the form is inadequate, the item should be continued on additional sheets, preferably 8½" x 11".

5. **FILING FEE** for this standard form is $3.00. If any other form is used, the fee is double.

6. Remove Secured Party and Debtor copies, and send other 3 copies with interleaved carbon paper still intact to the filing officer.

7. Fold only above or below TAB card copy for mailing. DO NOT bend TAB card.

8. At the time of original filing, the filing officer will return second copy as an acknowledgment. If acknowledgment copy is to be returned to other than the Secured Party or Assignee, please enclose a self-addressed envelope.

APPENDIX C
FORM OF CONTINUATION, ASSIGNMENT, TERMINATION, PARTIAL RELEASE, AND AMENDMENT

The following forms have been reproduced with the permission of and through the courtesy of Steck-Warlick Company, Austin, Texas.

70 **Uniform Commercial Code—FINANCING STATEMENT CHANGE—Form UCC-3 (Rev. 9-71)**

"LITHO-SNAP" • • • LITHOGRAPHED BY STECK-WARLICK CO., AUSTIN, TEXAS • • •

IMPORTANT—Read instructions on back before filling out form

This Financing Statement is presented to a Filing Officer for filing pursuant to the Uniform Commercial Code		3. Maturity Date (if any):
1. Debtor(s) (Last name first) and Mailing Address:	2. Secured Party(ies) Name and Address:	4. For Filing Officer (Date, Time, Number and Filing Office):

5. This statement refers to original Financing Statement No. ______________ Date Filed ______________, 19____

6. A. Continuation ☐	B. Assignment ☐	C. Termination ☐	D. Partial Release ☐	E. Amendment ☐
The original Financing Statement is still effective.	The Secured Party of record has assigned his interest in the following collateral to:	The Secured Party of record no longer claims a security interest under the Financing Statement	The Secured Party of record releases the following collateral:	The Financing Statement is amended as set forth below:

7.

By ______________________ By ______________________

Signature(s) of Debtor(s) Signature(s) of Secured Party(ies)

(1) Filing Officer Copy—Numerical

STANDARD FORM—FORM UCC-3 (REV. 9-71)—APPROVED BY THE SECRETARY OF STATE OF TEXAS—FORM 15-1556—THE STECK-WARLICK CO., AUSTIN, TEXAS

INSTRUCTIONS

1. PLEASE TYPE this form. Do not write in Box 4.

2. Fold only above or below TAB card copy for mailing. DO NOT bend TAB card.

3. This form must be signed by the Secured Party of record. If an assignment is presented along with the termination, however, the Assignee may sign this statement as the Secured Party of record. This form need not be signed by the Debtor unless collateral is added by amendment.

4. If the space provided for any item on the form is inadequate, the item should be continued on additional sheets, preferably 8½" x 11".

5. FILING FEE for statement specified under 6 A, B, C, D, or E, is $3.00. If any other form is used, the filing fee is double.

6. Remove Secured Party and Debtor copies, and send other 3 copies with interleaved carbon paper still intact to the filing officer.

7. At the time of filing, the filing officer will return second copy as an acknowledgment. If acknowledgment copy is to be returned to other than the Secured Party or Assignee, enclose a self-addressed envelope; however, if the Financing Statement is terminated, the acknowledgment can only be returned to the Secured Party of record.

APPENDIX D
INFORMATION FORM

The following forms have been reproduced with the permission of and through the courtesy of Steck-Warlick Company, Austin, Texas.

Uniform Commercial Code—REQUEST FOR INFORMATION OR COPIES—Form UCC-11 (Rev. 9-69)

52477

"LITHO-SNAP" • • • LITHOGRAPHED BY THE STECK CO., AUSTIN, TEXAS • • •

IMPORTANT—Read Instructions on back before filling out form.

Debtor (Last name first) and Address:	Party Requesting Copies or Information (Name and Address)	For Filing Officer

☐ Filing officer please furnish certificate giving the following information concerning any presently effective financing statement filed pursuant to the UCC naming the above named debtor and any statement of assignment thereof. See Fee Schedule on back of part 3.

☐ Filing officer please furnish exact copies of each page of financing statements and statements of assignments listed below which are on file with your office pursuant to the UCC. See Fee Schedule on back of part 3.

FILE NUMBER	DATE AND HOUR OF FILING	NAME AND ADDRESS OF SECURED PARTY

CERTIFICATE: The undersigned filing officer hereby certifies that

☐ the above listing is a record of all presently effective financing statements and statements of assignment which name the above debtor and which are on file in my office as of ______________, 19____ at ______________.M.

☐ the attached ______ pages are true and exact copies of all available financing statements or statements of assignment listed in above request.

______________________ Date

______________________ Filing Officer

(1) Copy 1

STANDARD FORM—FORM UCC-11—APPROVED BY SECRETARY OF STATE OF TEXAS—FORM 15-1536—THE STECK DIVISION, AUSTIN, TEXAS

INSTRUCTIONS

1. PLEASE TYPE this form in black.

2. Remove copy of party requesting information or copies (part 2) and send other 2 copies with interleaved carbon paper still intact to the filing officer.

3. FEE SCHEDULE: If request for information or copies is made on this standard form the filing fee is:

   INFORMATION:

   $5.00 for the certificate (however, if the number of statements reported therein exceed 10, then the fee for the certificate shall be $5.00 plus $1.00 for each statement over 10).

   COPIES:

   $1.00 for each page copied, but not less than $5.00.

4. No request for information or copies will be certified without payment of the total fee in advance. In order to expedite this request, it is recommended that a minimum of $5.00 be sent to the filing officer along with this form.

5. If this standard form is not submitted as a request for information or copies under the Uniform Commercial Code, the fee will be double that shown in the above schedule.